Youth Leadership in Action

A Guide to

Cooperative Games and Group Activities

Written by and for Youth Leaders

KENDALL/HUNT PUBLISHING COMPANY
4050 Westmark Drive   Dubuque, Iowa 52002

Acknowledgments

The Authors of this book would like to acknowledge and thank the following people who were important members of our team:

- Our families for their support and encouragement throughout the three long years;

- Colleen Tormey and Ari Russell for their contributions to the Sample Programs section;

- The people at Project Adventure's Vermont office for allowing us to use office space and computer equipment for the writing and editing process;

- Jim Grout, Kelly Brigham, Lynn Bedell and Tracey Dickson for their feedback on the manuscript;

- The administration, custodial staff and Steve "Hummer" Holmes of Brattleboro Union High School for sharing classroom space for photo, writing and playing sessions;

- Brattleboro photographer Robert McClintock for lending his skills and talents to the project;

- Our "models" for the photo shoots, which often included members of the Brattleboro Area Leadership Project Team;

- Tom Zierk, Project Adventure's publications director, for his enthusiasm for the original idea, his guidance and leadership throughout the writing process and for seeing to it that our efforts resulted in the book that you are now reading.

From Steve:

I would also like to make a special acknowledgment of the contributions of the young authors. This was, in essence, a volunteer effort with each of them contributing hundreds of hours. In July of 1990 Roger, Robin, Sanu, Jessica, Barbi, Abe, Susan and Zach agreed to lend their expertise and energy to my idea for the book. We did not appreciate the length of time that it would actually take to turn this idea into a finished product, yet for three years each has stuck with it and contributed fully. On behalf of myself, Project Adventure and everyone who will benefit from this book I extend a huge thank you to the eight of you.

Contents

Preface

There are four very exciting things currently happening across the United States and in other places around the world:

1. Teachers, parents and other community leaders are recognizing that young people are more than tomorrow's leaders — they are leaders today, capable of being valuable resources in schools and communities.

2. Delinquency, drug abuse, school dropout and other problems of young people can be effectively dealt with by giving them meaningful opportunities to contribute to their school and community.

3. Educators, business people and community leaders are recognizing that experiential (activity-based) education can help students make important connections between what they are learning in school and the world in which they live and work.

4. Leaders in all types of professions are recognizing that in order to be effective, their organization needs people with strong cooperation, communication and group decision-making skills.

But all too often young people have little access to the resources necessary to improve their skills and develop their leadership potential. There are volumes of material written for adult leaders along with training programs, seminars and conferences. If adults are truly going to commit to using young people as resources, we also need to provide them with the skills and tools to do the best job possible.

Youth Leadership in Action addresses this need. Designed as a how-to guide for youth leaders, it was written by and for young people to implement experiential, cooperative activities and programs. Combining the magic of Project Adventure activities with the power of young people leading them, *Youth Leadership in Action* also provides information on leadership skills, successful programs and directions to the activities.

We hope this book demonstrates the partnerships that can exist between young people and adults. Several youth leadership groups that Project Adventure works with in the United States and Canada are leading Adventure activities as part of their community prevention, school restructuring and/or youth leadership programs, and their efforts are really making a difference. Through the publishing of *Youth Leadership in Action*, we hope to provide many more youth leaders with a tool to help their programs get even better too, and to *Bring the Adventure Home!*

Introduction

Since 1971, thousands of outstanding teachers, counselors, camp staff and other professionals from all over the world have had a common experience — they have attended a Project Adventure training workshop to learn how to enhance their program by using cooperative, experiential and challenging group activities. Tens of thousands more have bought Project Adventure books to get ideas and learn activities. There is one other thing that these people have in common — they are all adults.

This book is designed to help you, a youth leader, *Bring the Adventure Home* to enhance a youth program that you are now part of or to start a new one.

Youth Leadership in Action is for you if you are:

- a member of a peer leadership group
- a youth group advisor
- a captain of a sports team
- a teacher using cooperative learning techniques
- a school group looking to do a community service project
- a Student Council member
- a recreation director short on staff but full of capable young people
- a student who would like to see more student-faculty collaboration
- a camp counselor
- an educator looking for creative ways to involve young people in teaching
- a young person wondering, "What can I do to make a difference?"
- an adult who counsels youths using methods of empowerment
- a member of a religious youth group
- a Scouting troop member
- a YMCA Leader or youth member
- a youth leadership trainer or conference organizer
- a young person looking to start or improve a youth leadership program
- an adult looking for a proven way to provide young people with meaningful leadership roles
- a young person looking to have fun and to share it with others
- a person who never considered herself a leader but who wants to explore the power of saying, "I can do this!"

In other words, this book is for anyone who wants to encourage cooperation, communication and understanding.

Youth Leadership in Action will introduce you to Project Adventure's philosophy and activities, show how other youth leaders have used these activities in a variety of different programs, discuss some issues that need to be looked at before you work with a group, and provide you with directions to 54 Adventure activities. All of these sections are important to helping you develop a great Adventure program or use Adventure activities in your current program.

On their own, the activities are a lot of fun to play. Our hope, however, is that you will get a sense of all the things that can be accomplished by using the activities in this book: things like cooperation, teamwork, communication, and increased self-confidence. But to help make all this happen, you need to have a firm and clear understanding of some basic Project Adventure ideas. That's why we have intentionally put the activities section toward the back of the book. Before you get there you will find sections on the history and background of Project Adventure, a description of just what we mean by *Adventure*, some fundamental goals, key concepts of Project Adventure programs and samples of youth-led Adventure programs (Chapter One). Chapter Two presents a detailed discussion of important leadership issues. Chapter Three provides categories of the different activities.

While we recognize that you are probably more excited about leading a group of twenty-five people through a session of *Everybody's It* than sitting and reading for a couple of hours, we strongly recommend that you carefully read through these sections. Doing so will ensure that when you do begin leading the activities you will give the group the best program possible.

There is also a short article on The Leadership Project. Since we mention The Leadership Project a lot throughout the book, we felt it would be nice to include this article, which first appeared in *New Designs for Youth Development* (Associates for Youth Development, Tucson, AZ, Fall 1989). We share this information with the hope that, like the rest of the book, it might open up new possibilities for your current program or help you to start a new effort. You may not be focusing your energy on substance abuse prevention, but we think you'll find the content useful for a variety of youth leadership programs.

Enjoy the reading and have fun putting it to use!

How Youth Leadership in Action was Written

By Steve Fortier

I believe that the story behind the writing of this book is an interesting and inspiring one.

Youth Leadership In Action is unique in several ways. For Project Adventure it is unique in that after years of training adults to lead our activities and programs, we are now helping youth leaders to use them. And while many youth leadership programs are designed to help young people work with their peers, this book is unique because it provides young people with a program that they can use to be positive forces in their communities, working with adults as well as their peers.

What we at PA are most proud of, though, is that *Youth Leadership In Action* was written *by* youth leaders. Most youth leadership guides are designed and written by adults. The gaps in language and experience between the adult authors and the youth readers can create challenges for the youth leaders as they interpret the writing and develop their programs. We wanted to avoid this by having young people with experience in leading Adventure activities write this book. What comes across are the experiences and understandable language of eight youth leaders. The students wrote all of the activity directions, and they wrote about their experiences using the activities in a variety of settings. The adults involved in this project have kept their input to a minimum because it would have changed the overall feel and tone, making this just another adult-written book.

The Writing Process

When we began this project in July of 1991, we had no idea that it would take three years to complete. For the first few months, we met one night every other week for two hours. By February of 1992, we decided that we needed more time and began meeting every week. Since not every group member was familiar with each activity, we did the activities before we wrote the directions. Besides having everyone learning all of the activities, there was another important reason for doing them. Just as you will use the activities in this book to help a group to communicate and cooperate better, doing the activities helped us become a high-performing team. This was especially important since the group represented all different ages, 11 to 18 years for the youth leaders and 28 for me.

We chose four activities to be written up for each week's meeting. Whoever knew an activity well would lead it for the rest of us. After doing these four activities, we would break up into two-person cooperative work teams to do the writing. Each team would pick one of the four activities and write the directions. We would have a 6th or 7th grader (Sanu, Jessica, Roger or Robin) team-up with an 11th or 12th grader (Barbi, Susan, Zach or Abe). After the activities were written, we started the editing process. During this phase we broke into pairs again to read the write-ups that other people had done. We were checking for clarity, to make sure no important points were left out, and to be sure all safety issues were included.

We also had to organize photo shoots to get photographs for the book. We wanted pictures of a mix of people enjoying themselves while playing the games. The Brattleboro area Leadership Project Team, headed up by Sue McClintock, was nice enough to allow us to take pictures at their Family Adventure Day in the spring of '92 and during a few Team meetings in the spring of '93. We also held photo shoots with middle and elementary school-aged youths that Sanu, Jessica, Roger and Robin got together. With the exception of a few lucky shots, the photos were taken by Robert McClintock, a professional photographer from Brattleboro.

All told, the creation of this book involved fifty or more people: parents, "models," editors, photographers, families, contributors from other parts of the country, and PA staff. It was this support and assistance that made this project, like all cooperative efforts, a great experience for everyone involved.

Author Biographies

The bulk of the writing of this book took place between July of 1991 and September of 1992. Between then and now we've all changed or graduated from schools, developed into new leadership roles in our schools and communities and just plain gotten older. Here's where we were at when we began and where we're at on this day in February of 1994.

Barbi Burrington

Barbi graduated from Brattleboro Union High School in 1993. She was a member of the Brattleboro area Leadership Project Team from 1989 to 1993, and was also involved with the Community Prevention Partnership as a youth representative. Barbi is now attending Aurora University in Illinois where she is majoring in Therapeutic Recreation. She's a member of Delta Phi Alpha sorority. Her future plans include working in the Adventure field (hopefully with Project Adventure!!!). Barbi says she enjoys seeing the difference that a group of people can make when they all work together for a common goal.

Steve Fortier

During the writing of the book Steve was co-manager of Project Adventure's Community Development Strand of programs and services. Over the past seven years, he has helped thousands of youth and adult leaders to use group activities as a way to develop partnerships between people. Steve was one of the creators of The Leadership Project, a program of Project Adventure that helps young people and adults Link Up to create healthier communities, schools and families. Steve now works with a training and consulting company in Far Hills, New Jersey which focuses on corporate teambuilding, community health promotion and youth leadership. He has earned a Masters Degree in Organization and Management from Antioch New England Graduate School and both a B.S. in Fitness and Health Management and an Associates Degree in Chemical Dependency Studies from Keene State College. Steve's family consists of his wife Susan, son Sean and daughter Laryssa. In his free time, Steve races bicycles on both the road and mountains.

Robin Conrad Frehsee

As a fifth grader Robin was a member of the Academy School Leadership Project Team. Robin is now an eighth grader at the Brattleboro Area Middle School where he is currently on the Board of Directors at the Brattleboro Teen Center. He enjoys mountain biking, skiing and playing the piano. Robin is also into art and takes photography lessons. He also wants to let you know that he loves cows.

Susan Henry

Susan Henry was involved in the Leadership Project at the Brattleboro Union High School for three years. She has also interned with Project Adventure and co-facilitated a ropes course Adventure camp. Susan is now a sophomore at Mount Holyoke College pursuing environmental studies and experiential education. It is her sincerest hope that everyone who reads this book really enjoys it and laughs a lot.

Sanu Mishra

Sanu is currently a ninth grader at Brattleboro Union High School. A member of Academy School's Leadership Project Team in sixth grade, Sanu likes to read all types of books and is an editor for a student literature booklet called DIAL. She is also a member of the BUHS chorus. Sanu was born in Nepal and moved here when she was four.

Zachary Pichette

Zach graduated from Brattleboro Union High School in 1992. He was a member of The Leadership Project from tenth through twelfth grades and really enjoyed using Adventure learning with elementary school classes. Working with the younger students in schools and as a camp counselor got him interested in being an elementary school teacher. Zach is now in college studying elementary education and plans to use Adventure in

his classroom when he gets a teaching job. In his spare time, he enjoys archery, water skiing and listening to music — particularly the Vermont band Phish.

Jessica Taft

Jessica is a ninth grader at Brattleboro Union High School. She is a member of the Brattleboro area Leadership Project Team and was a member of the Academy School Leadership Project Team in the sixth grade. She plays the oboe and, like Sanu, is involved with the DIAL project. Jessica is a member of the BUHS Drama Club and recently wrote, produced and directed a play and has acted in several others. She spent part of the summer between middle and high school backpacking in the Adirondacks. She enjoys reading and eating chocolate covered espresso beans.

Roger Thomasson

Roger and his family moved from West Brattleboro to Vestal, New York toward the end of the book-writing process. When he lived in Brattleboro, Roger was a member of the Academy School Leadership Project Team. He now attends African Road Junior High School, in Vestal, where he is a member of the football and tennis teams. He also plays the trombone and enjoys mountain biking and downhill skiing.

Abe Wilson

Abe is a 1993 graduate of Brattleboro Union High School. He was a member of the Brattleboro area Leadership Project Team from eighth through twelfth grades. While on the team, he led many Adventure programs for adults and young people, including co-leading Challenge Ropes Course activities. He also loved Dialogue Nights and presentations to younger children. Abe has been interested in the medical field since he was fifteen. He is now an EMT and works for a local ambulance service while also continuing as a ski patrolman, which he has done for four years.

Section One

Getting Started

1

Chapter One

An Introduction to Project Adventure

To help you understand and use the games, activities and ideas in this book, we would like to share some background information. This chapter will describe Project Adventure — how it began, some if its goals and a couple of its most important concepts. We will also try to answer the question, "Just what do you mean by *Adventure*?" This chapter will also provide examples of how other youth leaders are using Adventure activities in different types of programs.

A Brief History of PA

Project Adventure began in a Massachusetts high school in 1971. The first programs created were for physical education and academic classes. The idea was that if students could cooperate and work together, they could learn better. The students in the original program worked in groups on class projects, like studying a wetland and making a report to the town. To help them learn how to cooperate and work together, and to help breakdown cliques and build self-confidence, these students participated in different types of cooperative and non-competitive games and activities. Many of these were made up by the Project Adventure staff and were done during PE classes.

The original program was a great success and Project Adventure soon learned that other groups could also benefit by using their ideas. Many camps, recreation departments, counseling and psychiatric clinics, business people, college students and outdoor centers now use Adventure games and activities developed by PA. And in the places where it originally started, PE programs and school classrooms, Adventure programs now exist all around the country.

PA mostly trains others to use its programs. There are over one hundred workshops each year around the US, in Canada and in other countries. Project Adventure is also the world-wide leader in designing and installing Challenge Ropes Courses and sells many of the leading textbooks and games books used by people in the field of Adventure Education. Check out the back of this book to find out how to get their mail order catalog, which has lots of stuff for Adventure programs (from rubber chickens to climbing ropes).

Development of The Leadership Project

Started by Project Adventure in 1986, The Leadership Project was created to help communities deal with the problem of alcohol and other drug use by young people. PA teaches that groups who cooperate, communicate, and have fun together can overcome great challenges. So the Leadership Project puts together teams of young people and adults who work together to create healthier communities. These teams start programs to break down cliques, get people and organizations to cooperate better, and to give young people more opportunities to make a positive impact in their schools and communities.

One of these programs is youth-led Adventure. This program is a powerful way to use young people as community resources. We, the authors of this book, have led Adventure programs for our own school's teaching staff, the local police department, parenting classes, at community festivals and events, and as part of other programs that we offer. Our involvement in writing this book is a direct result of our relationship with the Brattleboro Leadership Project.

But Just What Is Adventure?

While the word *adventure* gets many people thinking about bungee jumping, white-water rafting, exploring the Amazon or rock climbing, Project Adventure believes that adventure can be found in more common places. If you want to have some fun, get a dictionary and look up the word, adventure. Most dictionaries describe it as "a noteworthy event or a remarkable occurrence." Some larger dictionaries also define adventure as an event that causes excitement and surprise. This is what Project Adventure means by *Adventure*. It means trying something new, that you didn't think you could do or might be uncomfortable doing. It

*Adventure comes
in many forms…
like trying something
different or new.*

is the excitement of playing, of having fun or solving a problem with a group of people.

The games and activities in this book produce different feelings for different people. This is where the Adventure comes in — for some, Adventure may come from holding hands with other people in the group in order to play *Impulse*. For others, speaking up to share an idea during a problem-solving activity will be their Adventure.

Some people will be uncomfortable at first with the silliness of some of the activities. But don't forget that within all the fun and silliness there is a lot happening to the group. The cliques are disappearing and people who may never have spoken to each other or thought they didn't like each other find themselves working and laughing together. Keep this in mind as you continue reading and learning how to lead the games and activities in this book.

Goals and Key Concepts

While Project Adventure has grown from a high school program to an international company, many of the goals and basic concepts are the same today as they were in 1971. We want to describe a couple of these goals and concepts that we think are important and because they will help you do a better job of leading the games and activities.

Goals

To increase the participant's sense of personal confidence.

Project Adventure believes that people are often more capable than they think they are; that they can do more than they think they can. The supportive atmosphere of the activities and your encouragement as a leader will help many participants try new things and be more involved than they may be used to. By doing this, participants gain self-confidence and begin to improve decision making skills, learn how to better communicate with others and come away with a feeling of, "Hey, I did it!" Some of this increased sense of self-confidence will remain with the participants long after the games are over.

To increase cooperation, respect and support within a group.

Project Adventure believes that if a person *tries,* that is reason enough to cheer him or her on. In these activities, winning and losing is not nearly as important as just playing, participating and having fun. In many cases, the success or failure of the group depends on the full participation of *all* its members. A group that cooperates and is supportive tends to get everyone playing, which means that the group is more likely to succeed. Trying new things can be difficult for anybody, but if participation is encouraged and valued over winning and losing, you can help participants begin to learn how to deal better with the tough parts of taking risks and trying new things.

Key Concepts

The Full Value Contract

One of the most important concepts used by Project Adventure is called the Full Value Contract (FVC). It is one of the things that really sets their programs apart and is a big piece of all the activities and games. Simply said, the FVC is an agreement made by all the members of a group that they will respect each other; that they will *fully value* all members of the group. It sounds simple, like the saying, "If you can't say something nice, don't say anything." But it means a lot more than that.

The Full Value Contract has four main parts:

1. The group is committed to the group goals and any individual goals that have been shared.

2. Group members agree to keep things safe — both physically and emotionally. The physical part says that we won't knock each other around when playing an activity like Link Up Tag. The emotional part says that we agree not to hurt anybody's feelings.

3. No put-downs — of others or ourselves.

4. The group members agree to speak up if they feel that another person did something that got in the way of the goals of the group or an individual. Remember though, that all members respect all other members, so if one participant tells another that he is not upholding his part of the agreement, it is done in a positive way.

Based on our experience of leading many different groups, we find the following short statements to be a good way to communicate the Full Value Contract to the group:

- Everyone needs to be committed to having fun.

- We don't want to hear put-downs of others or ourselves.

- We do want to hear people speak up (in a positive way) when they feel like cooperation, respecting each other and other goals are not happening.

- We will give positive encouragement to individuals and the group.

- All members will give 100% to the group effort.

- If people don't feel up to doing a particular activity, the group will allow them to sit out, but they may still encourage participation in a supportive way.

- Listen to the rules and for when the leader says *Stop*!

- Keep it safe — the activities are only fun when *everyone* is safe.

The exact wording here isn't important. But we don't start an activity until everyone in the group has agreed to follow these guidelines. The best way to do this is to have the whole group make some sort of statement right in the beginning of the program. Something simple like, "I agree to work with the full value contract," works pretty well for us. Or,

As the Adventure leader, you need to be sure that all group members understand and agree to live up to the Full Value Contract during your program.

people can just say, "I agree," or even just nod their heads. If someone cannot agree, ask the person why. Ask others in the group why they think the agreement *is* important. This positive peer pressure works well and we have never had someone in a group who could not agree to follow the FVC.

The Full Value Contract can also be very useful during the debrief (discussed in Chapter Two). By using the main points of the agreement, you can frame the debrief around questions like, "Did you hear any put-downs? Did everybody play safe?" We have also included an activity called *The Being*, which is an great experiential way to have a group develop their own Full Value Contract.

Challenge By Choice

Another important concept Project Adventure uses is called Challenge By Choice. This statement means that all participants choose their own level of challenge. Or more simply said, nobody is forced or pressured into doing something they don't want to do. It does *not* mean though that somebody in the group can choose not to participate at all in the program. You should explain right at the beginning that all activities will be done using this concept and that all participants have the right to pass on something they don't feel good doing. If a participant chooses not to participate in a particular activity, try to find another way for that person to be involved. Maybe he can help referee or keep count or score. What often happens in a case like this is that the reluctant participant sees how much fun everybody else is having and quietly enters the action. One of your roles as an Adventure leader is to encourage everybody in the group to participate at some level.

Putting It All Together

To briefly review, the goals and key concepts are:

- To Increase the Participant's Sense of Personal Confidence;

- To Increase Cooperation, Respect and Support Within a Group;

- Challenge By Choice;

- The Full Value Contract.

These goals and concepts are keys to running a successful Adventure program. By using them together, you will be a more effective Adventure leader, the groups you lead will have more fun in a safe way, and the participants will take some useful things home with them from your program.

Knowing how to use the goals and concepts is where your leadership comes in. If you, as the youth leader, keep these goals and concepts in mind, the group will naturally follow your lead. If you explain that your program uses the Challenge By Choice concept and then offer enthusiasm and support to the group, even the most shy and reluctant people will soon join in the fun. But they will do so on their own because they see that this is a group that cares, supports and encourages the efforts of its members. This is where self-esteem and confidence are built, and where your program of fun activities and games can have a lasting impact on the participants.

The next chapter discusses how you and other youth leaders can practice these goals and concepts and also have fun doing it by actually doing some of the activities. This teaches you how to run the games and activities before your group shows up, and it also gives you time to understand use the goals and concepts.

A Brief Word on *FUN*

You will find the word *fun* throughout this book — and for good reason. We believe that the personal and group goals of the people you work with can be accomplished best when there is a lot of joy and laughter. The non-competitive and cooperative nature of the games and activities get people having so much pure FUN that they forget the silliness, forget how they look, forget that some of the people they are playing with are from different cliques or don't hang out together. When you are having as much fun as these games and activities cause, it's easy for people to just let go and not really think about what is happening. Then when it's all over, some of those good feelings will remain — and that's what it is all about.

Sample Youth-Led Adventure Programs:

We feel that it would be helpful to provide you with some sample programs that we are aware of. We have deliberately included a mix of programs. The time frames of programs mentioned range from one-day to on-going. The settings range from a national conference to a fifth-grade classroom. The objectives range from improving cooperation within a school to teaching life skills. We offer these examples as a sampling of what a few other youth groups and individuals have done to combine Adventure and youth leadership. Don't feel that you have to copy any of these examples. We hope they will help to spark some thinking and creativity. The possible uses of the activities are endless.

Many of the examples provided come from Brattleboro, Vermont. And there is good reason for that. Brattleboro has many youth-led Adventure programs because this has been a focus of Project Adventure's Brattleboro office for the past few years. But we also were very fortunate to get examples from two people outside of our geographic area. Steve was introduced to Colleen Tormey of West Long Branch, New Jersey, by her Physical Education teacher and PS Cares advisor, Ed Kelly. Ed told Steve about Colleen and the other youth leaders on PS Cares while he was at a training workshop. He was told about the fantastic job Colleen does leading Adventure Games in her peer education program and called her to ask if she'd tell others how she does it. Steve met Ari Russell, the director of the Georgia Teen Institute, while attending a national prevention conference. They got to talking about what each of them does for work and Ari told Steve that she trains her junior counselors to lead Adventure Games as part of the Institute. Luck strikes again! The contributions of Colleen, Ari and the youth leaders from Brattleboro provide some exciting examples of the many wonderful things that happen when Adventure and youth leadership are mixed together.

The off-the-wall but always FUN nature of the activities encourages participation by all the participants.

One last time — keep in mind that we offer these examples to spark some thought for you of different places and programs where you might use the activities in this book. You will have different ideas and that is the beauty of Adventure games; people of all ages, physical abilities, men and women, living in urban and rural communities enjoy and can benefit from your Adventure program. Get creative with how *you* use them.

Peer Education Programs
contributed by Colleen Tormey
Shore Regional High School, West Long Branch, NJ
Class of '92

Adventure Games! You can find them in many places at my school. I was first introduced to them in gym classes. Now I lead them in my PS Care groups (the PS stands for Peer Support). PS Care is a peer support group that is run through our health class. We use Adventure Games to try to build self-esteem and self-confidence in teens. We try to get them to do something they never thought possible, within a group of their peers.

One day during my senior year, I had planned to play *Group Juggling* and *Moonball* to see if my group would cooperate well. My group consisted of about ten juniors, myself and the Principal. It was at the end of a long week and we wanted to just have some fun. We went into an empty gym and started to play. Our first game of *Group Juggling* went well. Mr. Kelly, one of our advisors, had given me some really neat stuff to throw around. We had some small stuffed animals, a koosh ball, some fleece balls and my personal favorite, a rubber chicken. We have the best time with that rubber chicken!

Our next game was *Moonball*. We had set our goal at fifty taps, which was pretty high considering we couldn't get past twenty for the first couple of tries. We talked about what we could do to get better. We decided that we would all really concentrate and not goof around anymore. We started back up again and we were doing better until someone hit the ball too softly and it hardly went anywhere. All of a sudden the Principal went diving to the floor to save it! We were all so stunned that we just stopped and watched the ball hit the ground along with the Principal. We helped him to his feet and continued with a lot more determination. I guess we all figured that if the Principal was that committed to helping us succeed then we could all try a little harder.

Along with the other students who run the PS Care groups, I am a member of the Teen Leadership Core. We were chosen for our leadership qualities inside and outside of school. As part of our training to become PS Care facilitators, we learn to lead Adventure Games. We usually start off our meetings with a game or two. We might do *Impulse* a new way, *Human Knot*, or our favorite, *Traffic Jam*.

The Teen Leadership Core uses Adventure Games in other places, too. We have held Peer-Parent Nights where we invite our parents to participate in some of the things that we do. They were always asking what we do at our meetings, so we showed them. We have also held "Play Days," where people can just come in and play games with us. One of our biggest accomplishments was our first Dialogue Night (ed. note — also developed by Project Adventure). It took a lot of planning, but it was well worth it. We have since gone on to hold other Dialogue Nights including one with our neighboring town's Drug and Alcohol Alliance.

I have found that Adventure Games can be played anywhere, with anything, at any time, with anyone. They can be used inside or outside of the school. That's the real beauty. You won't believe the great times it can bring you. It is also a great way to break down many barriers between people. And never be afraid to fail; half the fun is the challenge of leading the activities.

Vermont Department of Education HIV/AIDS Workshop
contributed by Barbi Burrington

The HIV/AIDS Workshop took place in October of 1991. The workshop was for teachers, school administrators, health educators and nurses from schools in southern Vermont. In all there were about 85 people.

Steve Fortier was asked to come and teach some Adventure Games to the group. He was also asked to speak about using young people as resources in trying to prevent AIDS transmission. Rather than talk about it, he decided to show them. So we (Abe and I) each led a group through some games that are aimed at improving decision-making and problem-solving skills.

First, as a big group, we played *Have You Ever*. Then, we split into smaller groups and played *Toss A Name Game*, *Warp Speed*, *Group Juggling* and *Balloon Frantic*. We ended with a large group *Fire in the Hole* by having everyone get in one circle and put their balloons on the backs of the people in front of them. They had a great time trying to pop all of the balloons!

The adults were all very impressed with the games and the way that we led them. It was different to lead a group of adults and I noticed that they had a longer attention span than the groups that we usually work with. I think that the Adventure Games alone would have given these educators some new ways to teach decision-making, but I hope that having two teenagers leading the activities taught them an even more valuable lesson — that young people are concerned about the issues that we are faced with, and that we can not only teach other young people about them but we can teach adults, as well.

Summer Camp
contributed by Susan Henry

Last summer I actually got a real job. I was to spend the next four weeks of my summer being a counselor to kids, aged 6 to 14. How in the world was I supposed to keep them entertained? As mud wrestling and swamp hikes were immediately ruled out, I thought... Adventure games! Great games for people of any ability. The games don't require all out brute force or promote competitive attitudes. The games instead encourage communication and fun. Perfect.

The campers arrived on Sunday afternoons, and each cabin spent the evening doing activities that helped the kids to get to know each other. Most of the kids didn't know their cabin-mates, so anything to get them talking was great. *Toss-A Name-Game* and *Have You Ever* were both wonderful games to get the them talking and, more importantly, laughing.

Before both lunch and dinner the whole camp assembled at the flag-pole. It was a time to bring everyone together and get focused before they flooded into the dining hall. *Circle-The-Circle* was a perfect game because it involves everybody. There were usually one or two campers who thought it was impossible, but by the time we had done it twice they were the most enthusiastic about breaking the previous 36-second record. Another game we often used was *Impulse*. After doing it a few times, the campers would usually suggest new and more difficult ways to try it. "How about with our hands crossed sending the impulse two ways?" or "Let's try starting the impulse at different places at the same time."

Once a week, the entire camp came together for an evening of more traditional games like Kickball, Frisbee and British Bulldog. Usually, the younger kids would opt to sit out because, "The big kids were so rough." We decided to reorganize, and yet again, Adventure Games came into the picture. The tag games like *Everybody's It*, *Link-Up Tag* and *Pairs Tag* worked really well. Depending on the boundaries we set, we were able to keep the group under control. (The "no running, but fast walking" rule is also a great way to control a large group of very excited kids.)

I used Adventure Games a lot. They were games that everybody could play and didn't exclude one age group from another. The games proved once more that there is more to life than winning and that maybe laughter is a little more important.

Center for Substance Abuse Prevention Training Workshop
contributed by Barbi Burrington

In October of 1992 I attended a workshop in Kentucky that was sponsored by the Center for Substance Abuse Prevention, a federal government organization. I was part of a twelve-person team representing the Brattleboro, Vermont area Community Prevention Partnership. I am a student representative to the Partnership.

At the end of the first day they had us play a closing activity. I could tell right off that what they wanted to accomplish with this game was not going to happen. Because I knew many games that would have worked to meet the goals, I said something to one of the trainers. They decided to have me lead an activity or two during the week-long workshop.

On the morning of the third day they asked me to lead a game. I had little time to prepare, no equipment and no PA books to help me generate thoughts of what to do. But I came up with a game and it went well.

I think my ability to match activities with goals and to quickly think of activities to do comes from having led and played many games. This book will help others to have that ability. There is a great feeling in watching people enjoying themselves and knowing that you created their enjoyment.

Academy (Elementary) School Leadership Project Team
contributed by Sanu Mishra and Jessica Taft

The year we were in the sixth grade, our fifth and sixth grade classes had a bunch of choices for community service projects and The Leadership Project was one of them. Our school counselor had seen the programs that the high school students on The Leadership Project Team were leading and wondered if we could do similar programs at the elementary school. So, he and the staff from Project Adventure got together to brainstorm what could be done. They decided to try the youth-led Adventure Games program. We chose to be part of the Leadership Project Team for our community service project.

Steve Fortier was the Project Adventure staff person that our school hired to help train us to do this program. When we were being taught the basics, like learning the directions to the games, Steve always seemed to remind us that having fun was always a priority. We had lots of fun and played lots of games like *Hagoo*, *Asteroid Tag* and *Speed Rabbit*. We also learned leadership roles and how to lead the games.

Then, we went into some of the younger kids' classrooms and led some games without help from Steve or other adults. The kids were always eager to play non-competitive games. We started off in each class by asking what communication means. The first and second graders also had some great ideas about cooperation. We were astonished at some of the kids' answers. They gave their ideas and thoughts openly. They mentioned things like teamwork, togetherness and helping each other to get something done. Then, we led the classes in activities like *Circle The Circle*, *Impulse* and *The Human Knot*.

We had one first grader who came up with a new version of *Impulse* using the tapping of feet instead of the squeezing of hands. Everyone laughed, had lots of fun and learned something, too. We learned a lot, but mostly we had lots of fun. Hopefully we helped some younger kids have fun, too.

Georgia Teen Institutes
Contributed by Ari Russell, Director

The Teen Institute (TI) model for actively involving teens in prevention has been around for over twenty-five years. The agency that I work for conducts the Georgia Teen Institutes. Each year, we conduct two TIs — one for middle school teams and one for high school teams. Community teams are comprised of five to ten students and at least one adult. Everyone participates in general sessions, elective workshops, social and recreational activities, and small sharing sessions called Family Groups. Teams meet throughout the week to assess the situations in their home schools and communities and develop action plans to address specific problems.

Since we began conducting TIs in 1989, we have always had Junior Counselors (JCs) who serve as youth staff members. Initially the JCs were our in-house "enthusiasm-generators and crowd-controllers." Their responsibilities have grown substantially each year and, consequently, so has the success of our programs.

Adventure Games are used throughout our Teen Institutes and Junior Counselors are responsible for choosing and conducting them. During the JC training retreat, new activities and games are introduced to the trainees and they are invited to lead others that they know. In this way, everyone has a substantial repertoire from which to choose. They decide which activities and games will be used for the Opening Sessions, Family Groups, Crazy Olympics, community times and the Closings. They also figure out who is most comfortable leading which activities and divide the responsibilities accordingly.

This year, the Opening sessions were led by several JCs, while others mingled with the participants to help explain, initiate action or encourage participation. They started with warm-ups and get-to-know-you activities like *Birthday Line-Up*, broke into several large groups for *Circle the Circle*, and finished up with a huge circle for increasingly complicated renditions of *Impulse*.

Each JC is assigned a Family Group to co-facilitate with an adult. They lead team building Adventure Games as warm-ups at the beginning of each session. During the first session, each member pairs up by finding the person most *visually* different from him/herself. (By the end of the week, Family Group members process the fact that while we may *look* different on the outside, we have much in common the inside). Pairs get to know one another and then introduce each other to the group. JCs then initiate more get-to-know-you activities like *Toss-A-Name Game* to help people remember the information about one another. Other Family Group activities they lead throughout the week include *Shipwreck*, *Human Knot*, *Willow in the Wind*, *Everybody Up*, and *Rainmaker*. Family Group time is one of the most popular parts of the Georgia Teen Institutes. Members of diverse ethnic groups and areas of the state become close friends.

Another important *elective* responsibility for the Junior Counselors is conducting either an informational workshop or a three-part prevention strategies workshop. Usually JCs team up to plan and present these workshops. This year (1992), nine out of ten prevention strategies workshops were conducted by teams of JCs. *And* their evaluations were great!

We're always surprised by other teen institutes or similar programs that do not give teens opportunities to plan and lead. If we expect youth participants to take active roles in prevention when they return home, what better way to encourage this than to provide peer role models who lead activities, take risks and are proud to be part of prevention?!

All of our TI participants are given opportunities to plan the next summer's programs. At the mid-year reunions, JCs lead focus groups to determine what activities and workshops were most popular, what needs to be added or revised, and what the most pressing issues are that should be addressed. They also lead new Adventure Games to get a feel for leading them and to see how well they are received. TI gets better every year because of this youth input.

Do we believe in peer leaders and the power of Adventure Games to bring a diverse group together? YOU BET WE DO!!

Bellows Falls (VT) Union High School *"Spring Fling"*
contributed by Steve Fortier

In 1988, the first year of The Leadership Project's program development in Bellows Falls and three other communities, the local Leadership Project Team and BFUHS Student Council created the "Spring Fling." The school administration was not going to allow the annual Winter Carnival to be held any longer. There had been an outbreak of fights in recent years caused by the intense competition between classes.

The president of the Student Council, Rebecca Rice, was also a member of The Leadership Project Team in Bellows Falls. She approached me with the idea of changing the activities from being competitive to being more cooperative using the many Project Adventure activities that she had done as part of The Leadership Project. We also agreed that changing the name of the event would be important so that it was clear to everyone (students, teachers, parents and administration) that this was a totally new thing. We then organized a small committee of Student Council and Leadership Project Team members to work with us on planning the event.

The school administration gave the students the go-ahead and on March 26th about 250 people (half of the school's 500 students!) had a fun-filled day of games and activities that required them to work and play together to win points for their class. We kept a bit of competition by having each class compete against the others by awarding points for each event. The difference, though, was that we structured the activities so that the class with the most people participating in the event was the one most likely to win. In past years, activities like powder puff football and volleyball had allowed a class to pick its *best* athletes to represent them since only a few people could participate. With the Spring Fling we wanted to challenge classes to involve all of their members, so we set up the point structure to reward the classes that brought out the most people.

In order to encourage more student/faculty cooperation and communication, each team was made up of both students and teachers. We had teachers compete for the class that they had for homeroom. It was great to see teachers and students playing and solving problems with each other.

Another nice part about the day was that Student Council and Leadership Project Team members partnered up to co-lead each activity. This was a nice way to bring together two of the groups within the school.

A few of the activities that we put into the day to make it more cooperative included Project Adventure activities  like *Frantic* (with tennis balls instead of Balloons — see the PA book *Silver Bullets*), *Four-Way Tug-of-War* (also *Silver Bullets,* under the name *Unholy Alliance*), *Great American Egg Drop* and *Giants, Wizards and Elves*. The students also used traditional events like relay races, cribbage, weightlifting, ultimate Frisbee and ping pong, but most of the emphasis was on getting class members to work with each other as best they could.

The choice of activities was based on what would work best with large groups of people. There are many other activities that are in this book that we could have used. If you'd like to promote a school or community activity that encourages cooperation and participation, you could do something like the Bellows Falls Union High School *"Spring Fling."*

2

Chapter Two

Leadership Issues in Adventure Programming

Before you jump right in and start using the activities, we want to share some tips on leadership that make them more fun, meaningful and educational. There is a lot to think about before, during and after doing activities with any group. For example: You will learn that some activities work best with certain size groups, or at a particular time in the program, or with certain age groups. We will try to pass along some of the things we have learned from leading many groups of both young people and adults and also information that has been developed by Project Adventure.

Remember the goals and concepts from Chapter One? Just to be sure, here they are again:

Goals

To increase the participants' sense of personal confidence.

To increase cooperation, respect and support within a group.

Key Concepts

Challenge By Choice

Full Value Contract

All of the activities in this book use these goals and concepts. It is up to you, as the youth Adventure leader, to be sure that they are followed by the group members. Your actions, instructions and behavior will go a long way toward how the group behaves and what individuals take away from the experience. This means that before you attempt to lead the activities you must first understand the goals and concepts pretty well yourself. Once you do, you will be able to present the activities to your group in such a way that they will understand and recognize their importance.

Our main goal in this chapter is to get you started on learning to be a good youth Adventure leader. Learning to lead Adventure activities is really like learning anything else. To get you through the process, we have divided this chapter up into the following sections:

- Training and Practicing

- Planning

- Leading

- Debriefing

- Advisor's Role

- Leadership Issues: A Case Example

Training and Practicing

Before anybody goes out to perform anything in front of a group of people — from an athletic event to a music concert — they do two things — train and practice. The same is true here. Training and practicing will do several things:

- make you more comfortable presenting the activities to a group;

- make you more confident that you can handle difficulties that may arise;

- make your program go more smoothly;

- help your own group communicate and cooperate better;

- allow you to have more fun when you are leading the activities.

One of the basic ideas behind Adventure and experiential education says that people learn best by actually *doing* something. So, we think the best way for you to start is by doing some of the activities. And the best place to do this is with a group of other youth leaders who might also be leading these games. If that doesn't work for you, or if you are

Practicing with a group where you are already involved is the best place to begin getting comfortable with leading Adventure activities.

more on your own, get together a group of friends or even some other organized group to help you practice. You might ask around to find if any advisors, counselors, teachers, coaches, etc. have any experience leading Adventure activities. If you find somebody, recruit him or her to help with your training. Follow an activity sequence based on the make-up of this practice group — do the members already know each other, do they work well together, etc. (More on activity sequencing later.)

How long you spend practicing the activities before you try them with a group depends on how much time you have and how you will be using the activities. Ideally, you should spend about 10–15 hours practicing before you lead other groups.

■ ***Example:*** You, or you and your group, have been asked to spend an hour helping the incoming freshman class get to know each other as part of their orientation day. This is a short, fairly simple program that will use lots of icebreaker activities. You will want to practice some of these beforehand to look at how to sequence them and also practice your presentation style.

■ **Example:** You have been asked to lead some activities and explain their goals and purpose to a parents' meeting. For this type of program you are going to have to be much more familiar and comfortable with the activities and also with the goals and concepts. You may be leading more complex activities than you would in the example above.

These are just two examples of where youth leaders might be called upon to lead a program. You can see that programs come in different levels of complexity.

Besides just practicing the activities themselves and becoming familiar with them, use this time to practice the goals and concepts. Your practice sessions should model the behavior you will expect from the groups you lead. This is the perfect time to talk about and practice things like cooperation, communication, trust and valuing each others' ideas and opinions. It is also an opportunity to see the Full Value Contract at work. By following the principles of the FVC as you practice, you will become familiar and comfortable using it. You will then be more confident and comfortable when you present the FVC to the groups you lead and making sure the group members also understand and follow its concepts.

You should also practice your own leadership style — how you present the activities, the rules and the safety reminders. All of the youth leaders in your group should offer each other feedback on how they come across when presenting the activities. An easy-going, interested, knowledgeable, humorous style will make a big difference on how the group reacts to you and the activities.

As you continue reading this chapter and learning about things like sequencing, briefing and debriefing, remind yourself that you will also need to incorporate these concepts into your training program so that you become knowledgeable and familiar with them, too.

Planning

OK, you have practiced with other group leaders and you're all ready to lead a group of ninth graders through a morning of team building. But before you run out and start playing, stop a minute and think the whole session through. This is the planning stage, and without it your session may not go as well as you'd like.

Here are some things to think about before your group shows up:

- group goals
- age of the participants
- size of the group

Planning ahead with a co-leader helps you to be sure that you are ready when the group shows up.

- sequencing of activities
- where you will be doing the activities (indoors, outdoors)
- supplies and props needed for the activities
- length of time you will be with the group

Group goals might help determine which activities you select. With a group whose members want to get to know each other better, you would use lots of icebreaker and get-to-know-you kinds of games. Another group may know each other well but wants to work together and communicate better. In this case you would use more problem solving Initiatives. Discuss goals with the person setting up the program — teacher, coach, adult advisor — ahead of time to determine the appropriate activities to plan on using.

The **age of the participants** is important because what might be fun and interesting for a group of fourth-graders might not work so well for tenth-graders. You might use similar activities but change or modify the rules. How you present the activities and the language you use might also be affected. You might talk to someone familiar with the group, like a teacher, or even to some of the participants themselves to find out what types of things might be fun for them.

The **size of the group** will help you decide what types of activities you will use and also how many leaders you will need. Many of activities in this book give recommended group sizes. Some of the problem solving activities need smaller groups of 8–12 participants. Other activities get better with more participants.

A fairly simple but important concept to include in your planning is **sequencing.** This refers to the order in which you do the games and activities. Depending on the above factors of size, age and goals, you will do certain activities or types of activities in a certain order. Generally, we start off with get-to-know-you or warm-up activities. Which activities you actually select will depend on how well the group members know each other. Warm-up activities tend to get the group going and spark their interest in what comes next. But don't stop here — doing only this type of activity will not challenge the group as much as team building, communication and decision-making/problem-solving activities. On the other hand, if you present activities that are too challenging too soon, before the group members get to know each other or begin to work together, they may struggle with the activities and become overly frustrated. The activities selection section, Chapter Three, will help you determine which activities work best at what point in your program.

Where you will be doing the activities might sound obvious, but we want to mention it. A large group with a whole field to play in will be able to do a lot of running around. But a large group meeting in a classroom or cafeteria or some other small indoor space won't be able to be quite so active. A little imagination and understanding of the activities can go a long way to getting the most out of the space you are given.

If you plan to play *Moonball* you need to have a beach ball. If you plan to play *Quail Shooters Delight*, you better have lots of soft, throwable things like fleece balls and softies, and rubber chickens. If you plan ahead and make a list of games and activities to play, be sure you list the **props and supplies** you will need for those activities. Most Adventure leaders collect, over time, a *bag of tricks.* This contains lots of stuff to play lots of activities. Many Adventure leaders take great pride in the unusual collections of strange objects they have in their bags — rubber insects, weird balls, colorful, soft Frisbee-type things — anything unusual and fun that says to the participants, "We're going do to something a little different here." Check out the activities selection section for some ideas on how to get your own bag of tricks started.

Now that all of this has been said, we'll also tell you that *A* doesn't always need to lead to *B* which then leads to *C.* "Be able to plan but also be able to be spontaneous. You don't always have to follow a step-by-step plan," says Abe, but a good plan always needs to have a back-up. If you intend to hold your activity session outside, what will you do if it starts to rain? Do you have activities you can use indoors? Sometimes it's fun to play in the rain, sometimes not. Also, if you are not able to see the location ahead of time, have a back-up plan that includes activities that can be done in a smaller space than you've planned for.

■ Last Minute Details

Here is a good checklist to go over before your group shows up:

- Have I got the props and materials I need?
- Are my co-leaders and I clear on our plan of action?
- Is the weather what I planned on or do I need to go to plan B? Do I have a plan B?
- Does the space I've got work for the activities I have planned?
- Do I know what activities I want to do and in what order I am going to use them?

Many of us like to write our down our activities and the order we plan to use them on an index card and put it in our pockets for quick reference. Once you get an activity started, you can take a quick peak to look at what comes next.

Another important part of planning is to overplan. Some of us list back-up activities on the back of our index card. This is always great in case you run out of activities before you run out of time or if you need to change plans for any other reason.

Leading

You've got your plan, you've got your props, you've got your field space, you've got your group....AAAHHH! No, don't panic, now the fun begins. This is where your training and practicing pays off.

You've practiced, you've planned, you're ready... Lead!

By being well-prepared you should not be as nervous as you might otherwise be. Some youth and adult leaders don't get nervous at all, while some people who lead quite a few Adventure groups still get butterflies. You can be nervous and confident at the same time. Remember all the time you have spent training and practicing and planning. As Barbi says, "Be confident and they'll believe in you. They'll follow your directions if you look like you are confident." And as Karl Rohnke, president of Project Adventure and the inventor of many Adventure games and activities says, "An ounce of image is worth a pound of performance."

Co-Leading

We strongly recommend that you co-lead (share leading the group with someone else) any time that you can. By having two leaders, even with a small group, you will find it easier than being on your own. If one of you forgets to mention part of a rule or a safety issue, the other can jump in and bring it up. If it is a long program, having a sidekick will allow both of you to keep focused and energetic throughout the day. Co-leading also helps during the debriefing times. Because there are two sets of eyes and ears, the questions that each of you ask might be slightly different based on what you each saw and heard during the activity.

Adult Presence

Any time you're working with a people under 18 years old, you'll want to be sure that your adult advisor or the adult advisor/teacher/coach, etc. of the group you're working with is present during the entire program. They aren't there to be supervisors, chaperones, police officers or referees, but it is important for an adult to be there in case someone twists an ankle or bumps their head. Also, if group members are acting out, it is easier for an adult who has responsibility for them to deal with these people so that you can concentrate on leading the rest of the group.

Starting the program

Getting off to a good start is important for any program. We usually start with a quick talk — quick being the key word here. Trust that the activities will do the talking for you, so you don't need to talk for too long about fun, Adventure, cooperation, etc. If you get the group going with activities, they'll learn pretty quickly what the program is all about.

If it is your first contact with the group, welcome them, introduce yourself, tell them about the group you represent and let them know why you're there. This is a critical point: if you show enthusiasm and excitement in the way you present yourself, you will spread this same sense of enthusiasm and excitement to the group. In the introduction we might also mention that we'll be having fun doing different types of Adventure games and activities, but part of the fun will be in overcoming group challenges together and cooperating and communicating well.

This is the point at which you should introduce the key concepts of **Challenge By Choice** and the **Full Value Contract.** Again, you don't have to go into a long-winded explanation of either of these, but you do need to be certain that everyone in the group understands and agrees to live up to them.

If the group seems "antsy," try saying just enough to give

An adult present during your program can help take care of unexpected problems.

them an idea of what the program is about and who you are, then present a few warm-up activities. After a couple of games, call a break and continue with the background information.

Taking Control of the Group

Although young people are usually on their best behavior when they are about to do something fun and different, there is the rare occasion when a few people are not paying attention or are messing around. As you might expect, the bigger the group, the harder it is to get control.

One day Zach got a group of over one hundred elementary school kids to listen to him and do the activities he was presenting, so we thought that we'd ask Zach to share with you some of his thoughts on keeping the group tuned to you, the leader.

"You want to try to get control of the group early on. If people listen while you are talking, aren't hitting each other and do what you ask them to do (like "please get in a circle"), then you are in control. If you're having problems with some of these, you need to try to not let a few people spoil the experience for the rest of the group."

Zach suggests not getting rid of the people who are causing problems right off. Instead he feels that it helps him to explain that *everyone* needs to know what is going on so they can work together. "Make sure they understand that the activities won't work without everyone's participation and cooperation. It's important, too, for you to take your leadership role seriously and show the group through your actions and words that you are serious. This doesn't mean that you can't have a good time like everyone else, but it does mean that when people are not paying attention or are breaking some safety rules, you will let them know how this creates problems for you and the rest of the group."

Get control of the group right away. Your strong leadership will mean that everyone has a good time.

It has been our experience that youth groups listen to and respect youth leaders. The fact that someone close to them in age is providing the leadership of the program seems to keep misbehavior to a minimum. When it does occur, misbehavior usually centers around a few friends who are playing around while you are trying to talk. The simplest solution is to split them up. An activity like *Have You Ever...?* will usually do this, or you can split the large group into smaller ones, making sure that the disruptive friends are separated.

This is also a good place where having an adult with you at the program will help. Your job is hard enough without having to deal with a few people who are having a bad day.

These same rules apply for adult groups. It is important to show your leadership ability right off by getting them organized, clearly explaining what you hope to accomplish during the session, and getting right into the activities. Some of the adults in the group may not expect such strong leadership from a *kid* and may leave with a new appreciation for what young people are capable of.

Participating With the Group

Youth leaders often ask, "Should I be part of the group?" You'll need to find out what works best for you, but in most cases there is no reason you can't join in. Not only will you have more fun playing along with the group, but you will also present a positive role model of what leadership can be. Too often in this world leaders are thought of as people who tell others what to do. We recommend that leaders be more a part of the group. As our resident philosopher Abe says, "Be one with the group." In warm-up and get-to-know-you activities, your participation helps you and the group get to know one another.

However, we normally don't participate in problem-solving, decision-making or team-building activities. These types of activities are designed to challenge a group to work together to solve a problem or complete a task. The focus should be on the group's working together to do this. As Susan says, "Let people make their own mistakes — don't give them the answers." Use your own judgment when a group gets stuck and begins to get frustrated. They will look to you for help and clues to solving the particular problem. Assess their level of frustration and decide whether to offer a small hint or clue. In most cases, given enough time, someone in the group will eventually come up with a solution, so we recommend that you bite your tongue.

Flexing

After a few activities, you'll get a sense of what types of activities are working best for the group. You may need to adjust your plan a bit at this point — what we call *flexing*.

■ **Example:** You are working with a sixth-grade group that is nervous and fools around during *Impulse.* During *Everybody's It,* they are fine, but when you try *Circle-the Circle*, they start fooling around again. Maybe they are uncomfortable holding hands. You may want to skip other activities that involve holding hands and try them again later or even during another session.

Another time that you may need to change your original plan is if there are group members with physical or mental disabilities or who have health problems. Check with the group's teacher or advisor ahead of time to see if there is anyone in the group with physical or health issues that you should be aware of. By doing this ahead of time, you can talk with the group leader or the people with the disabilities to find what types of activities they can and cannot do. Often they can do a lot more than we would think possible, so it is important to not just rule activities out based on your prejudices. If you don't know of any disabilities ahead of time and suddenly find someone who is visibly disabled at your workshop, take time to meet with the person and the group leader (and your adult advisor) to see if what you have planned will work, if you can alter any of the activities, or if you can, add other activities that this person can participate in.

■ Giving the Directions to an Activity

It would be pretty boring if you just read the instructions to an activity to the group. The activities are done with creativity and fun in mind and so should the way you present them. Know the basic rules and how the game goes, then add your own personal flair to your presentation.

Because the activities will be new to most people, you need to be sure that the group understands your directions. Steve Butler, PA staff member and Adventure Games Guru, introduced the DADDA concept to us. This is a great way to remember how to introduce an activity, because DADDA is one of the first words that most of us learn as babies.

D) Describe the activity — an introduction and rules.

A) Ask if there are any questions — does anyone not understand the rules or instructions?

D) Demonstrate — some activities are more easily understood if you first demonstrate the basic movements.

D) Do it.

A) Adapt it if needed — add more rules, safety instructions or add a new twist to it.

By going through these simple steps, your group should know exactly what you're asking them to do before they get started. This is important since the activities are geared toward group success. A misunderstanding of the rules can create frustration and can keep group members from doing their best with the activity.

■ Ending an Activity

Even the best and most fun activity will get boring if you play it too long. In order to prevent this from happening, Barbi suggests being, "one step ahead of them. Every activity has a high point. After this be ready to move on." It's always best to leave them wanting to do the activity again.

If you can find a fun way to end an activity it will be less abrupt than just yelling, "STOP." With the directions to some activities we have included a fun way to end it. We're sure that you'll come up with others.

Debriefing

We have said in several places that while the activities are fun, they can also be meaningful and educational. When you have a group that has specific goals to work on, you want to be sure that the group members have an opportunity to reflect on what happened during an activity or during their session. Just because you see things happening during the activities, don't assume that the group sees the same things. **Debriefing** gives a group an opportunity to look at what it has done during the activities. It can be done after a particular activity or at the end of a session. For example, if a group goal is to listen to everyone's ideas before trying to solve a problem, you may want to stop at the end of that activity to talk about what happened. How did they do, did they listen to everybody? Take the opportunity to talk about significant events. Educators call these *teachable moments*. If you wait until the end of the day to talk about this it may lose some impact. At other times, particularly when you've got only a few hours (or less) with a group, it is easier to do a general debrief at the end of the session.

Debriefing at the end of a program can help the participants take home some valuable lessons.

Here are some helpful hints on debriefing:

- Sit on the floor or ground in a circle — make sure each person can be seen by everyone else. Do not allow any group members to sit behind someone else.

- Ask questions that require answers other than yes or no. For example:

  "How did you feel during (name an activity)?"

  "What was the highlight of the day/activity for you?"

  "What did you get out of the day/activity?"

  "How can the positive things that happened today be taken back to our classes, families, school, group meetings, etc.?"

  If you are to meet with the group again, you can ask, "What goals can we set for next time?"

- You may want to use a "Whip Around" to get discussions started. This is done by having each group member say one word that describes the day or a particular activity for them. Go around the circle, one person right after the other. We ask other group members not to make comments about anyone else's word (Full Value Contract) and let people pass if they want to (Challenge By Choice).

- You can also make the debrief into an Adventure activity by giving the group some arts and craft supplies to make a piece of artwork that shows their feelings about the day. Pipe cleaners, small balloons, straws, tape, glue, popsicle sticks and construction paper are all supplies we've used. The group can even form a *human sculpture* using all its members. This can give the group members a more creative way to express their feelings. While this is one of our favorite ways to debrief a day, we need to warn you that it does take quite a while to do — usually 20–30 minutes.

No matter what technique you use to debrief an activity or Adventure session, don't let it run too long. We find most groups can't keep focused for more than 20–30 minutes. Most debriefs can be done in half that time and still be meaningful. Debriefs that go longer usually move into a counseling realm, one that many adults and most youth leaders are not trained to deal with. Lead the debrief just like the activities — leave the group happy and excited for more. Susan feels it's important to have all members leave with a positive feeling, which leads to more interest and anticipation for the next Adventure session or other program you may be doing with them.

Advisor's Role

Most youth groups are overseen by an adult — an advisor, teacher, counselor, program director, etc. This role is critical for your group and program. But it is important for advisors to remember that these are *youth-led* activities, and that their role may be a bit different than they are used to. Here are a few suggestions:

- It is tempting for adults to want to get things started for the youth leaders. It is our experience that this is not necessary and, at times, makes it harder on the youth leaders who follow.

- The advisor needs to allow the youth leaders to take the responsibility of leading the activities. This involves some risk-taking on their part. They need to trust the abilities of the youth leaders.

- We've already mentioned that it helps to have an adult present if somebody twists an ankle or bumps heads. Without their presence your entire program might be jeopardized if somebody gets hurt.

- Your adult advisor is an important resource in helping get your program started. They have access to budget information and can get funding for training and materials you may need. Within a school setting, teachers and school counselors are aware of the procedures for getting your program into other classrooms and how to reserve meeting and playing space.

While the youth leader's way of presenting an activity or leading a debrief may not be the way the adult would do it, he or she must recognize

Your adult advisor should act as a resource, not the leader of the program.

that a young person leading instead of an adult has many benefits. The adult, however, needs to understand the boundaries to this authority and control given to their youth leaders. Where the physical or emotional safety of group members is at stake, the adult needs to step in and help to set up safer conditions or deal with any problems that arise.

Lastly, the adult is there to provide support for the youth leaders. Like all good managers, your advisor

The Bumpers-Up position — arms bent at the elbows, hands out at chest height. We use this in many activities where participants are moving around and may bump into one another.

should be like a coach — preparing and helping you train to do the best job you can do, providing encouragement while you do your job, patting you on the back when it's over and providing you with positive feedback and ways you can improve.

⊕ Safety First

Wherever appropriate, the directions to the activities in this book include safety considerations. Project Adventure's Fifteen Year Safety Study, which includes thousands of programs, has found PA activities to be safer than both gym classes and organized sports. The reasons for this positive record include good training and great attention to safety.

Pay very close attention to the safety considerations listed with the activities. If at any time someone is not paying attention to the safety guidelines, you need to stop the activity. Deal with the person and the behavior that was unsafe. Remind the group of the Full Value Contract. If this person can't do things safely, you need to remove him or her from the activity or even the entire session.

Over time, a group will get better at sharing leadership, listening to one another and cooperating. But safety is something they have to be good at right from the start.

Leadership Issues: A Case Example

While you may not plan to use Adventure activities as they are used in this example, we wanted to "walk you through" the leadership issues that have been presented in this section.

Julia, an eighth grader, is a member of the Peer Leaders Group at Memorial Middle School. Her group has just finished a training program that took place once a week for an hour-and-a-half over a six-week period. The training program included topics like alcohol and other drug education, peer pressure and Adventure games. The training program was coordinated by Mrs. Sternberg, the Peer Leaders Group advisor. She did a workshop on leadership to kick off the training program. Representatives from the local police department and counseling agency did some of the presentations on alcohol and other drugs. Mrs. Bostwick, the Physical Education teacher at the middle school did the Adventure leadership training. She attended a Project Adventure workshop three years ago and uses games and activities throughout the year in her classes. Before the training program began, Julia had told Mrs. Bostwick about the Peer Leaders program. She mentioned that they were looking to do activities with other middle school students that would help to improve self-esteem and reduce peer pressure. Mrs. Bostwick volunteered to train them in using Project Adventure activities because she knew that these activities would help Julia and her Peer Leaders Group accomplish their goals. During the training program, Mrs. Bostwick talked about sequencing and debriefing and led the Peer Leaders through twelve activities that she thought would be useful in their program.

After the six-week training program was over, the Peer Leaders took turns leading activities as part of their weekly meetings. This practice gave them a chance to feel what it is like to be the leader and helped them work on giving the directions to an activity clearly. After each person led an activity, the other group members told them what they did well and what they might try to improve upon the next time.

Doing the activities also gave the group a chance to talk about how they could use them in their program. They decided that when they went to the classes in the school to teach their three lessons on alcohol and other drugs, they would start with a few games to get the students having fun. Jalen, an eighth grader who was a Peer Leader last year as well, mentioned that last year the students had been bored before they even started the classes just because the topic was alcohol and other drugs. He thought that a few fun activities like *Pairs Tag* and *Speed Rabbit* would be good to start each class with because it would get the students more "into" the program. Jenna supported Jalen's idea and also pointed out that those activities and others like them could work well in a classroom.

The Peer Leaders also thought that using the Full Value Contract would be a good way to talk about positive peer pressure. They also came up with the idea of using a few of the activities that Mrs. Bostwick had taught them as a way to get the students talking about other issues. Ian, a seventh grader, shared his idea of playing *Balloon Frantic* and then talking about how the group went about making decisions during the activity. He thought that the Peer Leaders could use this debrief to get the group to look at whose ideas were listened to and whose were ignored. He remembered from the training program on peer pressure that one of the main things that happens is that young people go along with other people's ideas or decisions without saying what they want to do or sharing their ideas.

Rather than have each pair have to go and buy balloons needed to do *Balloon Frantic*, Ryan, Lindsay, Laryssa and Katherine volunteered to get balloons and other supplies the group would need during their programs. Mrs. Sternberg made room in her office for the supplies. She knew that keeping supplies organized and easy to find would be important in helping the students run a great program.

The group also spent time writing and distributing announcements to all of the teachers at the school telling them about their program. They let the teachers know that they were prepared to teach three, one-hour classes on alcohol and other drugs and that the teachers should reserve time for the program by signing up in the teachers' lounge.

After a few weeks of practicing and planning, the Peer Leaders were ready to start teaching. Eighteen teachers had signed up for their program. The twelve Peer Leaders split up into six groups of two. These pairs would each lead three, three-week sessions. The group decided that they would pair up with diversity in mind. Most of the pairs had one male and one female and many had people of different races or ethnicity's. The group thought that since they would be talking about valuing all people, they should challenge themselves to work with someone other than their best friend.

Sean paired up with Julia. In the second session with one of the classes, they used Ian's idea of playing *Balloon Frantic* to lead into a discussion on peer pressure. During the activity the class members encouraged one another to share their ideas and listened to each of them before deciding what to do. Julia and Sean led the debrief with a focus on how everyone took responsibility for themselves and the group. Since they had introduced the Full Value Contract the week before, Julia asked the students if they had "fully valued" one another and themselves. One student talked about how he usually just goes along with what other people want to do because he is shy and afraid to share his opinion. He said that it felt really good to give an idea during the activity and to have the group try what he had suggested. He finished by saying that he would try to speak up more often when he felt it was important for either himself or a group of people. This led perfectly into Sean's presentation on peer pressure.

In the other eighth-grade class, this same part of the program produced a very different but equally educational, outcome. In this class a few people took charge and ignored the other people's ideas or put down them down. Three people told twenty-two others what to do. Some group members complained a little at the beginning but soon gave in to the three "leaders." After all, they were used to being told what to do by these three. This time Sean decided to do the presentation on peer pressure before getting into the debrief. He was afraid that without this information, the group members would not talk about what it felt like to be bossed around by others and not take responsibility for themselves. Following Sean's presentation, a girl quickly began the debrief by saying, "I didn't want to be the first to challenge the three people in charge, but if someone else had, I would have spoken up next." The young man beside her looked surprisingly at her and said, "I was thinking the exact same thing. I guess maybe next time we should do what Sean just said. We need to speak up for ourselves and know that other people will be there for us." Many other heads were nodding, as well. The discussion ended with one of the three saying, "I've been called a leader since first grade. I like being a leader and I guess I started thinking that being a leader means that you tell other people what to do. I've just learned that I can be a better leader by helping other people feel important too. That way, we all feel good!"

Conclusion

You, the Adventure leader, will shape and direct the group's experience. Your familiarity with the activities, combined with an understanding of the philosophy behind Project Adventure and your skills of sequencing, leading and debriefing will create a fun learning experience for all of the participants in your programs.

3

Chapter Three

Categories of Project Adventure Activities

Project Adventure goals can be reached through a variety of group activities. To help you choose the appropriate ones for your group or program, we have split them into different categories:

- Warm-Up
- Get-to-Know-You
- Teambuilding
- Communication
- Decision-Making/Problem-Solving
- Warm-Down

Each activity can probably fit into more than one category. For example, problem-solving activities also usually require good communication skills (speaking and listening). To simplify things, we have put each activity into one category where we think it can be best used. This lets you quickly pick out an activity that meets the goals of the group that you are working with. As you learn more about the different activities by doing them, you will get to know which ones can be used in different places other than where we have put them.

Warm-Up

Objective: To start off an Adventure experience. These activities are fun and allow group members to get comfortable with one another (if they don't already know each other) and give them an off-the-wall sense of what Adventure games are all about. These activities are primarily fun and group-based.

Features:

- Fun is the major component.
- They are success-oriented and can be done with little frustration — challenge is not a big part.
- They require little decision-making or problem-solving skills.
- Most require fast walking or other movement to *"get the blood flowing."*

Get-to-Know-You

Objective: To help group members learn each other's names and a little more about each other.

Features:

- Fun is a major component.
- Group members focus on learning about each other.
- As group members learn more about each other, they start to see that they really have a lot in common. This helps to break down cliques.
- Names can be learned in a fun (and fast!) way.

Teambuilding

Objective: Building on the opening activities, these provide an opportunity for group members to work together as a team and learn to value all the different members of the group.

Features:

- Once again, fun is a major component. Having fun helps to pull people together as a team.
- Since the activities involve problem-solving, the group begins to face challenges.
- Because of these challenges, the group needs to use *all* of its members well.

- Leadership tends to change hands during each activity.

- As leadership roles change, group members can see the strengths that different members have and that the *usual* leaders can't do it alone.

Communication

Objective: To provide an opportunity for group members to get better at communicating thoughts, ideas and feelings, and to improve listening skills.

Features:

- Require precise, descriptive words to solve the problem.

- Involve physical activity, talking and listening, and discussion.

- Require sharing ideas with others to help make group decisions.

- Solving a problem is the goal of the group.

- They allow leadership to come from the group.

- Most activities are done in pairs or small groups.

Decision-Making/Problem-Solving

Objective: To provide an opportunity for group members to communicate and cooperate with each other through activities that require the group to make decisions and/or solve problems.

Features:

- Physical activity, talking and listening are required to solve the problem.

- The problems require the group to try (and sometimes fail) and try again. This helps group members to learn patience and to not give up.

- Many times combining several suggestions will be the only way to solve the problem and do the activity well. No one person has all the answers.

- Leadership will change throughout the activity as different people have different ideas. This allows people who aren't usually seen as leaders to show that they have a lot to give to the group.

Warm-Down

Objective: To end the day's activities with a fun group activity.

Features:

- They build on the day's activities.
- Several of them can be talked about in relation to the theme of the day (cooperation, communication, having fun together).
- Participants leave the program with an up-beat attitude, feeling good about themselves and the other members of the group.

Activities By Category

■ Warm-Up Activities:

Ah-So-Ko	Hospital Tag
Asteroid Tag	Link-Up Tag
The Being	Pairs Tag
Comet Balls	Quail Shooter's Delight
Everybody's It Tag	Speed Rabbit
Hagoo	Whizz-Bang

■ Get to Know You Activities:

Categories	Toss-A-Name Game
Have You Ever?	Womp-Em
Peek-A-Who	
Robinjessicarogersanuabebarbiezachsusansteve (Name Impulse)	

■ Team-Building Activities:

Circle-the-Circle	Keep It Up
Don't Drop That Ball	Knee Slap
Everybody Up	Moonball
Four-Letter Word	Popsicle Pushup
Great American Egg-Drop	Quick Line-Up
Impulse	

■ Communication Activities:

Blind Polygon	Potential Problem Pit
Blob Tag	Tangrams
Hog Call	Traffic Jam
Line-Up	

■ Decision-Making/Problem-Solving Activities:

Balloon Frantic	Reverse Pyramid
Group Juggling	Two-by-Four
Human Knot	Warp Speed

■ Warm-Down Activities:

Count Off	People to People
Fire in the Hole	Rain Maker
Get Down	Texas Big Foot

Activity/Page	Space Needs		Props		Age Groups				Group Size			
	In	Out	Yes	No	Elem.	MS	HS	Adult	8-15	16-25	26-50	50+
Communication												
Blind Polygon (63)	•	•	•		•	•	•	•	•	•		
Count Off (78)	•	•		•	•	•	•	•	•			
FFEACH/MOOCH (88)	•	•		•	•	•	•	•	•	•	•	•
Hog Call (106)		•		•	•	•	•	•	•	•	•	•
Line-Up (118)	•	•		•	•	•	•	•	•	•	•	•
Potential Problem Pit (138)	•	•	•			•	•	•	•	•		
Decision-Making/Problem-Solving												
Balloon Frantic (58)	•		•		•	•	•	•	•	•		
Don't Touch Me (81)	gym	•	•		•	•	•	•		•	•	•
Group Juggling (97)	•	•	•		•	•	•	•	•			
Human Knot (111)	•	•		•	•	•	•	•	•			
Traffic Jam (156)	•	•		•	•	•	•	•	•			
Two-by-Four (159)	•	•		•		•	•	•	•			
Warp Speed (161)	•	•	•		•	•	•	•	•			
Wordles (169)	•	•		•		•	•	•	•			
Warm-Downs												
Chicka Boom (71)	•	•		•	•	•	•	•	•	•	•	•
Fire in the Hole (90)	•	•	•		•	•	•	•	•	•	•	•
People to People (134)	•	•		•	•	•	•	•	•	•	•	•
Rain Maker (145)	•	•		•	•	•	•	•	•	•	•	•
Texas Big Foot (151)	•	•		•	•	•	•	•	•	•	•	•

Section Two

Activities

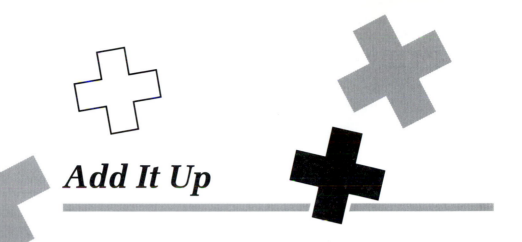

Add It Up

We certainly believe that there is great strength in a group that is diverse. In *Add It Up* the more diverse the group is in personal characteristics, past experiences and talents the higher their score for the activity.

Like many of the activities, you should feel free to create new categories that will work for the group that you are working with.

How To Play

- Break the large group up into "mixed up" teams of four to eight players.

- Give each small group one sheet with the categories and scoring.

- Give the group a time limit in which you expect them to complete the scoring of all of the categories on the sheet. We recommend not rushing them. With a long enough time limit (say a half-hour) the teams are more likely to listen and ask questions about exciting or interesting facts about each another. If the time limit is too tight, they will just say as much as they need to in order to get the scoring for the category.

- At the end of the activity, have the groups do as the title suggests and just *Add It Up*.

- If your group is not overly competitive, you can ask each team to report its score to the rest. If they are very competitive, rather than asking total scores you may want to just ask each group to tell everyone which category gave them the highest score or some other piece of information that won't get people saying, "Yeah, well we...."

Categories

To figure your Group Identity Quotient (G.I.Q.), add up your scores in each category.

Birthdays:

_____

Birthplace:

_____

Pedestrian:

_____

Intrepid Traveler:

_____

Celebrity:

_____

Adventures:

_____

Siblings:

_____

Surnames:

_____

Linguistics:

_____

Pets:

_____

Guidelines

1 pt.	for each **different** month
1 pt.	for each **different** state
( )	points for each shoe size, (TOTAL # of different sizes)
1 pt.	per person who visited one of the following: your state capitol, Washington D.C. or Disney World
1 pt.	for appearing in/on: TV, radio & newspaper (must be mentioned by name)
1 pt.	for: climbing a mountain, scuba diving, riding a roller coaster, doing a high ropes course
1 pt.	for each sibling (includes adopted, step, half-sibling)
1 pt.	for each letter used in anyone's last name
1 pt.	for each different language that a group member speaks well
1 pt.	for each different pet

Bonus Points

5 pts.	for anyone born on a holiday, leap year, or same day
5 pts.	for outside of U.S.
5 pts.	for over size 12 or under size 5
5 pts.	for each person who's been to **all** three
5 pts.	for each person who has been in **all** three media
5 pts.	for 3 of 4, 10 pts for 4 of 4
5 pts.	for multiple birth
50 pts.	for **all** letters, 5 pts. for each non-English letter
*	5 extra points for 3 or more
*	5 bonus points for each person who has more than three different types of pets

Ah-So-Ko

Ah-So-Ko is a great indoor or outdoor activity. We have never had a group not get totally into it.

Here is a story to help get the group into the right mood and to introduce the activity in a fun way:

> *Once upon a time, in a land far, far away, executions were very popular. The executioner would cut at the throat, the top of the head or just swing his sword and hit the person in the side of the head. There were specific noises let out for each type of execution. "Ah!" for the throat, "So!" for the top of the head, and "Ko!" for a swing at the side of the head. Since you'd probably get detention for cutting off someone's head, we won't use swords for this activity.*

By the way, this history may not be completely accurate. Susan heard it from her father, and he teaches science, not history.

How to Play

- Have the group sit in a circle in the traditional ancient lotus position (legs crossed in front).

- This game involves passing the three sword swipes and their noises in the correct sequence. The first person begins by saying Ah! while putting her hand under her chin. This player's fingers will be pointing at someone — either to the right or the left, depending on which hand she used— this player who is being pointed must make the next move.

AH!

- This next person must swing her hand over her head while yelling So! Again, the person who the So! player's fingers are pointing at is the next player to go. This participant can send the movement to the left or right (meaning she can send it to the next person in line or back to the person she got it from).

SO!

- The person who the fingers are now pointing at yells Ko! and makes a sword (hand) chop that points at someone anywhere in the circle.

- The person on the receiving end of this chop must start the sequence again with an Ah!, which of course must be accompanied by a sword chop below the chin and pointing to the left or right.

KO!

■ Rules

1) The sequence must always be **Ah!** then **So!** then **Ko!**

2) Whenever players make the wrong cry, make the wrong move (for example putting their hand above their head on **Ah!**), or wait too long while trying to figure out what they are supposed to do, they're out of the game.

3) Here's where the twentieth century, American aspect of the game comes in. Rather than politely explaining to the person that they did something wrong, the rest of the group pounds their fists on the ground, with their thumbs pointing up and all together they lift their hands up high while yelling, "You're outta the game!" The person who made the mistake must get up and stand behind the group of survivors. The survivors must slide closer together, filling the empty spot in the circle.

You're outa the Game!

4) The group member who was sitting to the right of the person who just got ejected from the game has only five seconds to start the sequence again with an **Ah!** If he or she fails to carry out this major responsibility… you got it — they're "Outta the game!"

5) The players who are out of the game are not really out of the game. In fact, their new role is at least as much fun as being in the circle. In their new role as "hecklers," they walk around behind the circle and try to confuse the other players by talking to them and trying to ruin their concentration. They are allowed to talk to the other players but they cannot touch them or block their vision.

Hecklers are still part of the action.

6) The game ends when there are just two players left. They are the *Ah-So-Ko* Champions — get it *co*-champions! Hey, what do you expect, we never promised a joke book.

Other Ideas

Groups usually want to play *Ah-So-Ko* over and over again because it's so much fun. One way to make it more difficult and a little different is to add a new movement. After the Ko person has pointed to someone, the person being pointed to has the option of doing Ah or they can hold up their hand like Superman blocking a bullet and yell **No!** This sends it back to the person who just did Ko who must start the sequence with Ah.

Another adaptation was recently developed by a group of sports captains Steve was working with in Bennington, Vermont. Rather than Ko as the final word of the sequence they used the name of the person being pointed to. (If the person beside me pointed to me while saying So, then I would do the hand chop to someone across the circle while calling that person's name). This is a great way to combine the fun of *Ah-So-Ko* with the benefits of a name game.

Asteroid Tag

Asteroid Tag is a high-energy, fast-action, heart-pumping, sweat-dripping (OK you get the idea) game. This one involves throwing objects as the "tag." Groups of young people (and many adults) love tag games. Add the throwing of things and the excitement level goes up even more.

Things You'll Need

Lots of soft things to throw — fleece balls, nerf balls, soft frisbees, etc.

How to Play

- Lay out a fairly large area so that there is lots of room to run around. For a group of young students or people with disabilities that might affect their throwing ability, a smaller area would be desirable. For a group of high school athletes, you'd probably want a large playing area to increase the challenge.

- Participants start out holding one soft object and when you yell "GO," they throw their objects/balls into the air.

- The game has now started. Each player runs around picking up the objects and throwing them at the other players. For safety, we always say that hits above the waist don't count toward getting someone "out," only those below the waist do.

■ Rules

1) People may pick up as many objects as they'd like throughout the game.

2) If you are hit, you are not permanently out. Instead you must throw all the objects that you have into the air as you did at the beginning of the game. Then you must kneel down.

3) When you are kneeling, you may not move. The only way to get back into the game is to catch a ball or pick up a ball as it rolls by. *Remember,* you can't move your body on the ground, you can only reach out with your hands! When you get an object that was going by, you can now return to the game. Just stand up and start playing again.

4) When balls are thrown outside the playing area, the player who threw the ball goes and gets it. While the person is outside the playing area, he or she is "safe" from being hit. (As the leader, make sure that people are going outside to get a ball and are then getting right back into the game.)

5) Since there is no winner (it's rare that only one person is left standing), it's a good idea to put a time limit on the game. There is so much running around in this game that 5 minutes is usually all that a group can take!

✛ Safety Note

One safety issue to be aware of is that people who are kneeling down need to keep their hands to themselves. Since people still in the game will be running around, they could easily be tripped by those kneeling down, which could obviously cause some accidents and injuries.

Balloon Frantic

Balloon Frantic is an excellent, colorful, fun and challenging problem-solving activity. It can be used with small, medium and large groups and with people of all ages (with some adaptations for younger students). *Balloon Frantic* does need to be played indoors.

Things You'll Need

Lots of blown-up balloons (at least one for every participant)

How to Play

- Every person in the group needs to have a blown-up balloon (the larger the better).

- When the leader says "GO," players hit their balloons up into the air. From this point on the group is trying to keep all of the balloons up in the air by hitting them with their hands or heads (no feet). Because this is a group activity, the players do not necessarily have to hit their own balloon (they can give theirs away and/or hit other people's), but all balloons must be hit and not held.

- The leader starts a stopwatch on "go."

- All the group needs to do is to keep hitting the balloons to keep them from hitting the floor. Easy!

- The only problem is… every 15 seconds the leader throws a new balloon into the game, which the group must keep up in the air like all the others.

▪ Rules

1) If a balloon hits the floor, the leader(s) screams at the top of his or her lungs — a simple "AAAAAHHHHHHH!!!!!" will do. When a balloon hits the ground it is called a *berserk*.

2) If that same balloon stays on the floor for five seconds without being picked up and put back into play, the leader screams again. A balloon that is just sitting there is called a *hectic*. Every five seconds that this balloon remains on the floor is another *hectic*.

3) After six screams, whether they be from *berserks* or *hectics* or both, the group has become *frantic* and the game ends. The leader will stop the watch and let the group know what their current World Record is.

Things to Think About

Give the group a minute or two to strategize for the next try and then get them started on an attempt to break their previous World Record. This is where the problem-solving part comes in. The group may decide they need to arrange themselves in a certain way or give people certain jobs like receiving all incoming balloons. Lots of neat ideas will emerge during this planning session. Some will help, some may not, so give the group a few chances to plan and try new ideas.

✚ Safety Note

Use only hands and heads to keep the balloons afloat — flying feet can be dangerous to other group members. Make sure that you are playing in a safe area with nothing to trip over or run into. Players will be looking up at the balloons, so they will not be able to look out for things they might bump into or trip over.

The Being

This activity is an active way of helping a group to develop their own Full Value Contract. *The Being* provides a group with some goals related to how they want to work together and some of the negative things that they want to avoid. Having *The Being* with you as you do other activities allows you to check in with the group on how they are doing with their group goals.

Things You'll Need

A 7-foot by 4-foot (or so) piece of paper (the rolls that most schools have in the art room work just great)

About a dozen magic markers or big crayons.

How to Play

- Start by having a volunteer to lay down on his back on the piece of paper. Be sure that his whole body is on the paper.

- Have a few players outline this person's body on the paper with the markers or crayons. Depending on the age and maturity level of the group, you can either draw the outline yourself or have the person lying down choose who he would like to do it.

- The outline of this player's body (or something like it) will be drawn on the paper when he gets up. This is *The Being*.

- Gather all the players around *The Being*. Give everyone a minute to think about what type of behaviors and attitudes would be helpful to the group and some that would not be helpful to the group.

- After a minute or two for thinking, place the pens so that players can grab them and ask them to each write inside the body at least one word that they would like to see as part of the way group members work together — common words are cooperation, listening, caring, involving everyone.

- There are also negative things that will get in the way of a positive group experience for everyone. Next have players write some words that they thought of that they do not want as part of the group because of their negative consequences — common ones here are everyone talking at once, put-downs, prejudice, not listening, not involving everyone, stereotypes.

- If you have a large group you will probably want to have each player write just one word on the inside and one on the outside so that you don't end up with a huge list.

- You can also have the group name their Being.

- Take time, once everyone is done writing, to go around and have people say what they meant by the word(s) they wrote down. This is important because there will be several words that mean slightly different things to each player. In order to work on them together, all players need to be clear on what the word means to the person who wrote it down and what it might mean for other players.

Things to Think About

Once completed, *The Being* provides a great tool to debrief an activity, a workshop, a day of activities, or an entire program of more than one day. Checking in periodically keeps the players focused on how they're treating each other. This is important because a lot of times the groups get so caught up in the fun and problem-solving of the activities that they lose sight of how they are acting. And, since they generated the list and it isn't just a bunch of rules that you (the leader) or the teacher or boss or someone else made up, the group is much more likely to use their *Being* to compliment each other on positive things and call each other on negative things.

If you are working with a group more than once, posting *The Being* in the room that you use is a great reminder and it also allows group members to add more to it as time goes on.

Other Ideas

Rather than a body, you can use other figures as your *Being* if you'd like. At a workshop that Steve and members of the Brattleboro Leadership Project Team led at Mount Anthony Middle School (Bennington, VT), we had students draw the outline of the school. The reason that we had been asked to do the workshop was that they were trying to set a positive tone for the new school year. Using the school helped us to talk about keeping good behaviors and attitudes in the school and leaving negative ones outside.

If you're only doing a one-time workshop, you can see if the group or teacher or group leader would like to take *The Being* with them. While you only have control of the group when you're with them, *The Being* can live on if the group uses it in settings outside of your program.

Blind Polygon

This is a great communication activity for a group of any age. We highly recommend it if you're working with people who often have to make group decisions together (student councils, school boards, etc.), because it forces people to speak one at a time rather than having fifty-five leaders all at once.

Things You'll Need

One rope long enough for all of the people in your group to hold on to

How to Play

- Blindfold all of the members of the group. If there are no blindfolds hanging around or if people don't want to use a blindfold, just have them close their eyes.

*Is this a square,
or a triangle trapezoid?*

- Place the rope on the ground near the feet of the group members and instruct them to find it. (As if the rest of the problem isn't hard enough!)

- Explain to the group that the object of the activity will be to first find the rope and then form it into different shapes. All group members must be holding the rope and therefore are part of the solution. They can talk to each other.

- Tell the group that the first shape they have to make is a square.

- After a while, ask the group whether they feel that a square has been formed. When greeted with a "no," let them continue, even if they *are* in a square! If the group thinks that they have made a square, have them take off their blindfolds or open their eyes. After looking at their "square," give them time (one minute) to discuss a plan for how they will work out the next shape that you give them.

Other Ideas

Other shapes you can use are: triangle, circle, rectangle or the game-ending triangle trapezoid. (We say "game-ending" because there is no such thing. If they start to try make it send them immediately to the geometry teacher.) If no rope can be found, this activity can be done by having the people hold hands.

One solution that some groups use is to move people around. This is perfectly acceptable to us but we would not mention it to them. If they ask if it's legal you can tell them yes, but let them get creative rather than giving them helpful hints.

Debrief Hints

If you choose to debrief this activity, a lot of leadership and communication issues usually come up. Depending on what happened to your particular group, a few typical questions might be:

- When was communication a problem? Why (were too many people speaking all at once)?

- Were any people or ideas not listened to? Why? How might that have hurt the group in trying to solve the problem?

- When did it get better? What changed to make it better?

- Who were some of the leaders during the activity? What did they do that might be considered leadership?

- Did what happened during this activity look anything like what happens in your group (class, student council or staff meeting, football huddle, counseling group, etc.)?

Blob Tag

Blob Tag is a very active game. It's most fun with a group of twenty or more and really needs to be played on a grass field because usually a few people fall down while playing. And because there is a lot of running, it should only be used with a group that has demonstrated that they are concerned about each others' safety.

How to Play

- Designate boundaries. Remember — you need a LOT of space for this one.

- Choose two players to start The Blob.

- These players either link hands or arms.

- The game begins and the two players, linked together as The Blob, try to tag other people.

- When players are tagged or go outside of the boundaries, they must link onto either end of The Blob by holding hands or linking arms.

- Only the players on the ends of The Blob are allowed to tag people because they are the only ones with a free hand (the outside one).

- The Blob must stay linked together in order to tag other players.

- The game ends when only one player has still not become part of The Blob.

✚ Safety Note

Do not yank on other player's arms. Remember, you are a very goopy blob and would fall apart if pulled too much. The rule of fast walking, no running can be used here. Maybe after the group has done this safely you'll feel OK about letting them run. The most fun game in the world is suddenly no fun when someone gets hurt, so do what you need to make it safe. An almost guaranteed way to have someone get hurt is to allow people to break through or dive under the middle of the blob. We don't allow this at all. The only way to safety is to get around the ends of the blob.

Boop

Boop is a great indoor activity to help with communication and cooperation. It works with any size group because you are splitting them into groups of three anyway. A large area, cleared of chairs, desks and other hazards is a necessity.

By the way, you may be wondering where the name *Boop* came from. Since we're into experiential education, blow up a balloon and hit it. Listen closely when you hit the balloon. Did you hear the sound? It said *Boop*, didn't it?

Things You'll Need

Balloons (blown up)

How to Play

- Begin by splitting the large group up into groups of three (a few may need to be four depending on the overall group size).

- Have the players in these small groups join hands. Give each group a balloon. Make sure that the groups are spread out enough to allow for some moving around.

- Each group tries try to keep the balloon up in the air (off the ground). They *must* keep their hands joined during the entire game. Give the groups a minute or so to practice. During this time let them use any body part that they'd like to keep the balloon up.

■ Rules

1) After a short practice time, you (the leader) call out a body part and that's what each group must use to keep the balloon off the ground.

2) You'll want to change about every ten to fifteen seconds during the activity. For example, you could start with hands only (one of the easier ones), move to heads only after fifteen seconds or so, then maybe elbows only, knees only, noses only, etc.

3) We like to move on to combinations after that, say head-hand-elbow. What this means is that a head shot must be followed by a hand shot, then an elbow shot and then back to a head shot, and so on. Have fun making up your own sequences, like nose-heel-shoulder.

4) Remind the groups that their hands must be joined at all times and that the balloons should never stop moving, even as you call out new body parts to use.

How many different body parts can you come up with for the group to use?

Other Ideas

You can set a playing time before you start (like 3 minutes). If the group is in a competitive mood, you can have the groups keep track of how many times their balloons hit the ground and compare at the end. If they're not competitive, you can just play without counting floor touches.

A fun way to end the game is to tell the groups to do the next command for as long as possible to see who the "winners" are and then yell, "No body parts at all." How in the world do you do that anyway? Ah... like all of these activities there is a way. Only problem is they've got to figure it out before their balloon hits the ground. (One way we've seen people do this is to blow them up in the air with their mouths.)

See *Fire in the Hole* (Page 90) for a fun way to end your balloon activities.

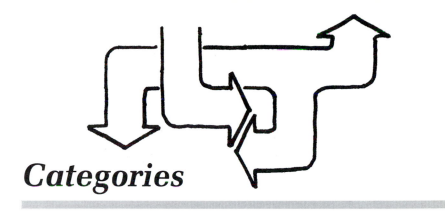

Categories

Categories is a great large-group activity where members can get a sense of what they have in common and also how different they are. It can also be used as a way to get people talking and learning each another's names.

How to Play

Explain to the players that you will call out a category and, as quickly as possible, they then need to get together with everyone else who belongs in the same category. It's as simple as that!

Some Categories that We Recommend

- Have everyone fold their hands together and then look down at their hands. If their left thumb is on top have them get together with everyone else whose left thumb is on top. All righties get together. Check it out. This is usually pretty close to a 50-50 split.

- Get together with everyone born in the same month.

- Left- or right-handed?

- Get together with everyone who has the same number of children in their family.

- Which leg do you put in your pants first? (Warning: This may result in three groups because some people put both legs in at the same time!)

- Same color eyes.

- Picture your toilet paper at home. Is the first sheet coming off the roll from the top or underneath?

- Same favorite fast-food restaurant.

- Do you use a comb, brush or nothing to fix your hair?

- Get together with everyone who has the same favorite color.

- What other categories can you think of?

Things to Think About

Like we already mentioned, this activity can accomplish two things at the same time. Give the group a couple of minutes between categories for people to meet each other, say "hi," or answer a question you'd like them to think about.

Chicka Boom

Because *Chicka Boom* is such a totally silly activity, we might save it for when a group has gotten used to the often silly nature of the activities. But don't get locked into this — if you and the group seem ready to jump into it, by all means "Go For It! *Chicka Boom* is also a real fun, no-purpose way to end a nice session of Adventure, which is why we put it in the warm-down category. As far as group size goes, any number will do, but the more the merrier.

You may want to tell the *Chicka Boom* story, or make up one of your own, before giving the instructions. The storytelling part adds to the Adventure of it all. Have fun with it.

Years ago there was an old storyteller named Chicka Boom, who would travel from village to village in Northern Peru. He was a wonderful old man who wove tales of fantasy and myth, constructing games from his imagination. His one joy in life was children. He loved children and would spend endless hours playing games with them. When it was time for the storyteller to move on, he decided to leave the village children the present of a game before he left. The game, named after the storyteller, is still played today by children everywhere.

(*Chicka Boom* may actually have been a PA instructor who clearly had too much free time on his hands if he could spend time thinking up this activity.)

How to Play

- Gather the group in a circle in a big open space.

- The leader stands in the center, and asks everyone to join in the song and dance by following his or her actions and words. After one verse everyone should know the words and steps.

- The leader begins the song and dance.

Go up Chicka Boom,
Chicka Boom...

Song: "Go up... Chicka Boom, Chicka Boom, Chicka Boom"

Dance: Hands pointing up towards the sky, going up and down with the beat. The feet also move, so that opposite foot and hand are moving at the same time.

Go down Chicka Boom,
Chicka Boom...

Song: "Go down... Chicka Boom, Chicka Boom, Chicka Boom."

Dance: Hands now pointing down, continuing motion with the feet.

Song: "To the right... Chicka Boom, Chicka Boom, Chicka Boom."

Dance: Hands pointing to the right, feet still moving up and down taking small steps to the right.

Song: "To the left... Chicka Boom, Chicka Boom, Chicka Boom."

Dance: Hands pointing to the left, feet moving up and down now taking small steps to the left.

Song: "Now you know where it's at, its a little of this and a little of that. So, come on in and get down."

- Now turn around and pick someone to join you in the middle. Both you and the player you picked now lead the group in another round of the song and dance. At the end of this next verse, pick two more people (one for each of you), and the four of you now lead it and then pick four more. Keep going until everyone is in the middle. Once everyone is in the middle, do one last verse.

Yahoooooooooo!

Yahoo!

Circle the Circle

This Adventure Hall of Famer encourages teamwork and problem-solving. People of all ages enjoy it!

Things You'll Need

Two Hula Hoops

A watch

How to Play

- Get the group into a circle and ask them to hold hands. If they complain, explain that cooties are out of season and there is no danger of catching them today.

- Place the hula hoop between two players so that their hands are through the center of the hula hoop.

- The object of this activity is to get the hula hoop all the way around the circle and back to where it started by somehow getting people through the hula hoop *without breaking hands*. Group members can help each other as long as they do not break hands with the people on either side of them.

- Let the group try it once without timing them.

- After the practice run, ask the group to discuss what problems they had and how they can solve them so the next try will go smoother.

- Ask the group to establish a time goal for themselves. This is a good lesson in group goal setting. If the group that you are working with is large and/or young, you, as the leader, may need to decide on a group goal using the input that the group has given you. We usually try to find an average of the goals that are suggested. (For example, if we hear 30 seconds, 1 minute and 3 minutes, we might suggest a minute and thirty seconds as a group goal.) In a smaller or more mature group you can let them establish a goal by themselves — a good group decision-making challenge. Either way, ask one last time if everyone understands and agrees with the goal.

- Try the game again and time it.

- If the goal is not met after this run, you may want to encourage them to try again using the same goal or setting a new goal. Either way, ask the group if they have any ideas of how they could improve upon the last time. If the group does meet their goal you may want to ask them to try to set a new one and try again.

Another Idea

After the group has had a few tries at *Circle the Circle* with one hula hoop, you can add a new challenge. Choose a starting person and put one hula hoop in this person's right hand and one in the left hand. People on either side of the starting person should grab his or her hands through the center of the hula hoop. On *Go*, the two hula hoops need to go in opposite directions around the circle. Both hula hoops must go around the circle and end up in the same hands that they started in. (The hula hoops will need to cross each other twice in order to successfully complete this). Remind the group — at no time can they break hands. This activity may be frustrating, but it always works out when people work together!

Comet Balls

These things are great. I had always called them shmerlofs. My father would take all of his old socks, put tennis balls in the ends, and tie them off, making these really neat things to launch around the back yard. The challenge for my sister and me was to try to get them over the house (my mom quickly stopped that game when we kept on missing and hitting the windows instead). Shmerlofs were also liked by dogs so when playing with them you might want to pick a dog-free area just for the sake that slobbery socks can get really disgusting.

What you do with your *Comet Balls* is up to you, these are just some suggestions. Be creative and have lots of fun.

Things You'll Need

Socks or nylon stockings and tennis balls (both can be old and well-used, but clean)

How to Play

- Play catch with a partner, trying to get farther and farther away with each throw. Catch the Comet Ball only by the tail. For really long throws, the Comet Ball can be swung around in a circle by the tail a few times before letting go. Perfecting your aim with this method takes some practice.

- Play horseshoes, using a bucket or hula hoop instead of a stake. Two of them placed about 25' apart works well.

- Make up you own games using Comet Balls.

- Have a blast!

Count Off

Count Off is a quick, indoor or outdoor, sunny day or rainy day activity that is sure to frustrate a group. Of course, they'll have fun while they get frustrated!

How to Play

- Have the group spread out in a small area. They should not be in a circle, square or any other pattern — just spread out. Have them facing all different ways just for good measure. Once people are settled in a spot, have them close their eyes.

- The objective of the activity is quite simple. The group needs to count from one to ten with the following rules:

▦ Rules

1) The same player cannot say two consecutive numbers (three and four, for example). A player can say more than one number, as long as they are not in order.

2) Any time two or more people say the same number at the same time, the group must go back to number one.

3) The group members cannot speak other than to say a number (they can't make a plan!).

Sounds simple, huh? Just wait. In the hundred or so times that we have led this activity, only one group has gotten from one to ten on the first try. Success or lack of success with this activity has little to do with how well or how poorly a group is working together. Make sure you keep encouraging the group as the frustration level goes up and try to get them to laugh at themselves between tries.

Each attempt at this activity only takes a few seconds, so let the group keep trying as long as they'd like. Some groups have been known to skip dinner and sleeping in order to get to ten (just kidding). They'll get it — it's only a matter of time!

Don't Drop That Ball

Don't Drop That Ball is a fairly challenging activity because it involves catching and throwing. Since it may lead to frustration, it is sometimes best saved for use after a group has succeeded at some other activities. Because of a lack of eye-hand coordination among elementary school kids, you may want to reserve this one for older groups. This activity can be done indoors or out and is best with groups smaller than ten to fifteen. If you've got more people than that in your group, you can split them up.

Things You'll Need

Lots of soft balls (nerf, tennis or fleece)

How to Play

- Starting with one ball, a player throws it about ten feet up into the air. Another player needs to catch it.

- If this was done without the ball hitting the ground, another ball is added so that two players now throw their balls into the air and two other players catch them.

- Each time a throw is successful, another ball is given to the group.

- All the balls must be thrown into the air at the same time and caught by someone other than the thrower. A thrower can throw a ball and still catch another person's in the same turn.

- If any ball is dropped, the group starts over again with one ball (too bad!).

Things to Think About

Let the group figure out their own systems (the way they spread themselves out, how they count to throw all together, who they want to catch, etc.). You can also give the group some time between throws to develop new ideas and plans. This can be interesting because sometimes groups will just keep doing the same thing with twelve balls that they did with one when maybe they need a new way of doing it.

Just a reminder that this activity may be challenging for individuals or an entire group, so be aware that frustration might develop. Every group needs to experience frustration, so we don't advise that you avoid using *Don't Drop That Ball* — just be sure to think about where you place it within your activity sequence.

Don't Touch Me

If you're looking for an active problem-solving activity, here's a great one. The other nice thing about *Don't Touch Me* is that it works well with both large and small groups and can be altered on-the-spot based on your group size. You do need a large playing area — field or gym.

Things You'll Need

Either a hula hoop or 6–8 foot length of rope
A stopwatch

How to Play

There are a variety of ways to present this activity, so we'll present the different options along the way in these directions. Experiment on your own with different groups to see which way you like to best present it. If you're doing a lot of leading, change it around from time to time for your own fun.

- Place the hula hoop or rope (shaped into a circle) in the center of your playing field or gym.

- Divide the group up into an even number of smaller teams. You decide how you'd like to do it. For example, if you have twenty people you could have two groups of ten, ten groups of two or four groups of five. Take your pick, any and all combinations will work for this activity as long as there is an even number of teams. Try to make each team have the same number of players, but if you have an odd number of people in the group, just make the teams as even as possible.

- Have each team pick a spot about twenty feet from the circle and spread them out evenly around the center. Each team needs to be lined up directly across from another team.

- This activity is timed. On your command of "Go," the members of each team try to get to the same place as the team across from them. They will do this by passing through the circle in the middle. Each member must put at least one foot into the hula hoop or rope circle as they pass through the middle on the way to the other side. The time for the entire group will be the time it takes for the last person to get to his or her new spot.

◼ Rules

1) Not only must each player touch a foot inside the circle, but for the entire time while they are passing through the circle, no group member can touch another. Each touch results in a five-second time penalty. A ten-second time penalty will result if anyone kicks the circle (whether it be a hula hoop or rope) causing it to move or change shape.

2) Give the group some planning time before their first attempt. Like in many activities, you can have a set planning time, like three minutes, or allow them to plan however fast or slow they'd like. Both bring up interesting discussions about how the planning time was used.

3) When planning is over, yell "Go" to begin the activity. Players cannot move in front of their designated spot until you've said, "Go." You don't need to say this (because you want them to come up with the idea), but if someone should ask, once you have said "Go," any group member can move toward the center. Players don't have to wait behind their line until it is their turn to pass through the center.

4) After the last player has gotten to his or her new spot, stop your watch. This is the group's base time. Now check for penalties — touches of people or the circle. Ask the group if there were any touches. Let them judge themselves. Most groups will expect you to be the tough judge. Asking them to tell you will bring up issues of honesty and integrity — "Do I speak up when I know I touched Sue if I know that this is going to add five seconds to our time? The group might get mad at me. Maybe no one else saw it. Sue won't bring it up will she?" Add up the time penalties, add them to the time it took them to complete the problem and you have the group's total time (and the current World Record!).

5) Give the group some more planning time before they have another go at it.

6) Depending on the group's mood, two, three or four attempts should leave them smiling and feeling accomplished.

✚ Safety Note

> You should encourage members to put "bumpers up" when they are going through the center. This is done by participants putting their hands up, about a foot in front of their chests, palms facing out. By doing this, even in the heat of action, group members will be able to just push off from someone in their path rather than possibly bumping heads.

Everybody's It Tag

Got a group that needs to burn some energy? Here's a fast-action game that works best with large groups, and is a sure bet to be loved by all the players. It is also an excellent warm-up because it gets everybody moving, hearts pumping — and it's a whole lot of fun! You'll need a good-sized, flat space to play in (a gym or playing field would be the first pick).

How to Play

Mark off a large square or rectangular area on a playing field or gym floor. Give the group the following directions:

- Spread out within the boundaries.

- Rather than having just one person be it (as in other tag games), everyone tries to tag each other in this game (hence the name *Everybody's It*).

- When tagged, players must kneel down where they are and remain kneeling for the rest of the game (don't worry, it won't be long — this is a FAST game!).

- The last person standing is the winner.

- Without giving the group too much time to think about the last game yell, "Go" again to start a new round. This game is a quickie and is fun to play a few times.

Things to Think About

Something that often happens is that two people argue over who tagged whom first. One way to deal with this is to make them negotiate, within five seconds, who is to kneel and who is still in the game. At the end of the five seconds, if they haven't resolved their conflict, they are both out.

Other Ideas

If two people are left in the game, you can add a rule that the first person to either get tagged *or* to take a step backward is out — this forces the players to go after each other and usually leads to a quicker ending.

✚ Safety Note

Walking only (NO RUNNING!). As the leader you should tell the group that anyone running will automatically be out of the game — and be sure to enforce this rule. With players running all over, it's impossible for them to watch out for each other, which leads to head knocking and unplanned body slams. The only way to avoid it — no running!

Tags should be made with hands only — no kicking — and tag gently.

When kneeling down, players need to keep their hands to themselves. Serious accidents and injuries can happen if someone gets tripped.

Everybody Up

This activity can be done with just two people or with a group of two to the sixth power or so. (Bet you didn't know you'd have to use what you learned in math class to figure out how to lead a game, did you?)

How to Play

- Players pair up, then sit down, facing each another with the soles of their shoes pressed against the other player's shoes.

- Now have them reach out and grab their partner's hands.

- By pulling as hard as they can, with their partner doing the same, the players try to pull each other up to a standing position.

While the directions seem simple, this activity is not so easy to do. Encourage people to keep trying and to think about what they can do to increase their chances of succeeding. Like some of the other activities, strength is less important than using a well-thought-out strategy.

Things to Think About

To begin with, letting players pair up with someone their own size makes sense — it will make getting up a bit easier to do. After a few people have been able to do it, though, have them switch partners to make male-female pairs or pairs of people of different sizes. If they've succeeded once, they should also be able to do it with different partners. By mixing people up like this, you can help people to change some of their stereotypes about the physical abilities of people of a different sex or body type.

Other Ideas

This game can also be done with a bigger group, just make sure that everybody's feet and hands are touching and then PULL!!

✚ Safety Note

For safety purposes, this activity should not be done in a classroom or on a hard floor. You want to be sure that there is nothing that someone's head can hit (desks, walls, etc.). Grass or mats are the best surface to do it on in case someone's hands slip and they fall backward.

OK, everybody puuuuull!

Ffeach/Mooch

Ffeach/Mooch is a Steve Butler original. Steve works with the Steve of this book in Project Adventure's Vermont office. *Ffeach/Mooch* derives its name from the first letters of the various categories involved in the activity. As you will see, the name changes with the categories.

This activity is a fun, slightly competitive game that can be played with groups of ten or more people. You will recognize it as a team version of the game Charades.

Things You'll Need

Your list of categories and words

How to Play

- Divide your group into smaller teams of five to ten people. Try to have an even number of people on each team. Like we have said before, use a fun activity like *Categories* to split the group up.

- Spread each group out so that they are equal distance from each other with each group being about twenty feet from you.

- Present the group with the following rules:

■ Rules

1) The activity begins with a representative of each team coming to you for a word.

2) The word you give them will fall under one of three headings. In the case of *Ffeach*, the headings are **F**ast **F**oods, **E**lectrical **A**ppliances and **C**omic **H**eroes. Just pick three categories, put the first letters of the words together and you'll have the name of the activity!

3) These first people will return to their group to act out or hum the word or phrase that they were given. These first people are the only ones who will have the same word at the same time, after that you will start to mix them up (to prevent a group from listening to another team's answers).

■ Comic Heroes

Roger Rabbit
Popeye
Garfield
Snoopy
Superman
Bugs Bunny
Donald Duck
Minnie Mouse
Roadrunner
Teenage Mutant Ninja Turtle
Fred Flintstone

■ Electrical Appliances

washing machine
vacuum cleaner
toaster
VCR
TV
stereo
trash compactor
air conditioner
fan
popcorn maker
hair dryer

■ Fast Foods

pizza
ice cream cone
taco
Big Mac
french fries
egg roll
hot dog
chicken wings
fried dough
onion rings

■ Psychological States

boredom
peace
ecstasy
frustration
fear
stress
joy
confusion
panic
relief
paranoia

■ Hums

Jingle Bells
Happy Birthday
Jaws
White Christmas
Star Spangled Banner
Born in the USA
Help
I can't Get No Satisfaction
I heard It Through the Grapevine
We Are the World
your school song

■ After School Activities

football
cheerleading
drama
marching band
computer club
student council
soccer
field hockey
track and field
detention
nintendo

■ Movies

Dances With Wolves
Sound of Music
Field of Dreams
Honey I Shrunk the Kids
Jaws
Animal House
Star Wars
Batman
Rambo
Terminator
Beauty and the Beast

■ Prime Time TV

Home Improvement
Cheers
Married With Children
20/20
Funniest Home Videos
Full House
Brady Bunch
MASH
Wheel of Fortune
Doogie Howser

■ School Classes

math
chemistry
phys. ed/gym
wood shop
cooking
sewing
art
music
American History

Fire in the Hole

This activity is usually used at the end of another balloon activity and is a fun way to dispose of the balloons.

Things You'll Need

Lots of blown-up balloons

How to Play

- Separate the group into pairs. Players will probably want to be with a good friend or someone they know well. Each pair needs at least one balloon.

- The pairs must be very close together and facing each other. They place a balloon between them, about chest high, and when the leader tells the group to start, each pair yells, *"Fire in the Hole!"* and hugs each other tightly enough to pop the balloons.

- Hands are off-limits, but chests, butts or backs will all get the job done.

- So that you're invited back again, make sure all balloon scraps get picked up!

Other Ideas

Fire in the Hole can also be done by getting a group of five or more people in a circle, all facing in one direction (so that one person's chest is facing the next person's back) with a balloon between each player. Again, after the warning, *Fire in the Hole*!, the group tries to pop all of

Squeeze!

the balloons. As we mentioned in the Sample Uses chapter, Abe and Barbi once did it this way with about 85 teachers. It was outrageous!

✚ Safety Note

This game could get rough without a lead-in about safety. Most often, the roughness is a nervous response of people who aren't comfortable with hugging. Since we are recommending this as a closing activity, you will have a pretty good sense of whether the group is responsible enough to handle *Fire in the Hole.* If not, the ol' "put it on the floor and stomp on it" method is probably best.

We don't recommend it for elementary or middle school students, but if that's who you're working with, you be the judge. As always, when you have any doubts, check with your advisor. High school students and adults usually get into it pretty quickly.

Four Letter Word

This is a super indoor or outdoor activity for large groups. *Four Letter Word* is also a great way for people to learn a few things about each other. Four Letter word works best with a group of at least 30 people, and is great for people ages 10 to 62. It's one of the most successful activities we've done with adults.

Things You'll Need

Lettered cards (see below)
A watch

How to Play

- Before your class or workshop begins, you need to make enough 3"x 5" cards so that each person gets one. It's a good idea to make a few extras. Once you've made them, stash the cards somewhere so they can be used again.

- Put one letter of the alphabet on each of the cards. If you are making just thirty cards, you may want to make one card for each of the letters from A to Z and four with a ✻ on them. The ✻ is a wild card and can be used as any letter. For larger groups, make more cards with vowels and other letters that are frequently used (s, d, m, l).

- Give each player one card. This is their letter for the duration of the activity. Once everyone has a letter, give the following rules:

■ Rules

1) After you yell, "Go" (or some other word of your choice) each player has one minute to find three other players who have letters that will spell out a four-letter word. These words must be clean (no swears). Give the group examples to help demonstrate, like: frog, wild, rain and team.

2) Again, the ✱ can be used as any letter. Whoever has one of these cards will probably make friends very quickly!

3) Once four people are together with a four-letter word, have them stand together with their hands up in the air.

4) After one minute yell, "stop!" — at which time everyone should stop where they are. If you are working with a large group, 50 or more, you may want to bring along a whistle or some other loud noise maker. Foghorns work well.

5) We like to take a minute or so to quickly go around and ask some of the groups what words they came up with. It is fun to see some of the words, and it recognizes these people for their hard work.

6) After you've checked in with some groups, yell "Go" again and a new round begins. Anyone in a group of four needs to break away and look for three new people to form a new four letter word. Again, everyone has one minute to do this.

7) We'll usually do five to eight rounds of *Four Letter Word* so that everyone has a good chance to get into at least one four-letter word group.

Other Ideas

When we use this activity as a way to help group members get to know each other better, we tell the groups ahead of time that at the end of the one minute period, we'll give them another minute to meet the other three people in their group. Encourage players to get each others' names if they don't know them yet. If time allows they could also talk about other things. This part is why *Four Letter Word* is such a nice way to help people in a large group get to know one another. All together, it is hard for thirty or sixty people to learn each others' names or a bit about each other. But, by breaking them into groups of four, this is easily accomplished. If you are going to give the small groups this minute to talk, make sure that you have first told people who have not gotten into a four letter word to make their own small groups so that they can participate in this part of the activity as well.

Don't forget to collect your letters when the activity is over and stash them away somewhere for the next time you play *Four Letter Word*.

Great American Egg Drop

The *Great American Egg Drop* is an extremely fun, group problem-solving activity. You should have a group of at least ten to twelve so that you can split players up into smaller work teams. We use this story to set the stage and get the group into the spirit of the activity.

Between WWI and WWII, the American Air Force was tackling the problems of air-lifting food to people in starving countries. The Air Force had particular difficulty with eggs and how to drop them from a plane without getting broken. If you are successful at this, the Air Force would be happy for your input, as they still haven't quite got it. (Nobody at the Air Force would respond when we tried to question them, so this may not be true.)

Things You'll Need

20 straws per group

30 inches of tape per group

1 egg per group

You'll also want a garbage bag, paper towels and a trash can for cleanup.

Different amounts of these materials and other materials can be used. Paperclips and rubber bands instead of tape are often fun to try.

How to Play

- Split the group into teams of four to six people.

- After giving each group the materials, instruct them to construct the safest "vehicle" for their egg to travel from a height of six feet to the ground. The objective is to keep the egg from breaking when dropped. The egg must be inside the vehicle somehow (the straws are not laying on the floor with the egg dropped into them).

Give the groups thirty to forty minutes to develop their egg-saving vehicles. Also during this time, each group must develop a name and a commercial for their product. Encourage them to develop a commercial that lets everyone else know why theirs is the best, most protective, most efficient egg-protector on the market. Groups will need to present their commercial just before dropping their egg.

- After 30–40 minutes get everyone back together in a large group. It's show time! Have them sit on the floor of the room in a horseshoe shape so that there is sort of a stage in the middle for the egg drops.

- See which group would like to be the first to do their commercial and drop their egg. Each group should have a representative drop their egg from a height of about six feet or just have them reach up as high as they can and drop it from there — sneaky groups will have their shortest person do it, while not so sneaky groups may have their tallest, which obviously makes the heights different but, hey, let them figure that one out.

- The surviving eggs go on to be dropped from a height of eight feet (by standing on steps or a chair), and increasing heights afterwards. For the super-duper egg protectors, you may need different stories in a tall building.

- The egg that makes it to the highest drop without breaking is the winner. Or, to have more than one winner (always a great idea so that more people can share the success), simply have one or two rounds and any non-oozing eggs are declared winners.

- As the judge, it is your job to look for a clear or yellow oozy substance trickling or flowing through the straws and onto the garbage bag or whatever you've set down. If you find this, it is a good indication of an embryonic hematoma, more commonly known as a scrambled egg.

Debrief Ideas

This activity can be debriefed with a bunch of different themes. Depending on the goals of the group, you could help them to look at:

Who did what — How did they divide themselves to do the construction and write the commercial? Did they decide who did what based on who wanted to do what or who might be best at each? Were some people left out of the process? Were the people writing the commercial those who got left out of the building of the vehicle?

Planning — Was there a common plan that everyone was committed to? Did they plan first or just start building? If there was no plan, would one have helped? Would it have saved time in the long run to have taken the time to hear suggestions from people and then develop a plan, as opposed to just doing, doing, doing? Did the group spend too much time planning and run out of time to complete the construction (we call this "Analysis Paralysis")?

Leadership — Who took charge and why? Did leadership change as the group went through the planning and building stages? Did anyone help to keep the group together and keep everyone involved?

Group Juggling

Group Juggling is an excellent introduction to problem-solving. It isn't heavy-duty challenging, but it does gives a small group of 8–12 players a chance to decide on strategies, set goals and work together on solving a problem.

Things You'll Need

Several fleece balls

Rubber deck rings

Other small, soft objects

How to Play

- Have the group form a circle.
- The leader(s) should join the circle as well and (at least for the first run) should be the starter.

- The first part of the activity involves establishing a pattern where one object will be passed around the circle so that each group member gets it once and it ends up back at the leader. The first person to go is the leader who throws it to someone else in the circle. No one can toss to someone right beside them; it must go at least two people away. An easy way for the group to remember who has gotten the object and who hasn't is to have everyone start with their hands out in front of them. As the players receive the object they put their hands down.

- Here's the important part — everyone needs to remember who they got the object *from* and who they threw it *to*.

- The final person to receive the object will be the leader who started it. Check in at this point, everyone in the circle should have gotten the fleece ball (or whatever you're using) once. It should have started and finished with the same person (the leader). OK? Good!

- Now that you have that pattern established, you will begin the actual *Group Juggling*.

- Begin by throwing the object to the same person you threw to in the first round. As soon as that person has passed it on to the next player, add another object. And another. And another. And another… get it?

- Continuing with the same pattern, the group will be *juggling* several objects at once. As soon as an object has gotten all the way through the pattern and back to the leader, keep the game going by again throwing it to the next person in the established order.

- Many objects will go sailing by players and get dropped or collide in mid-air — just keep adding more. The group may want to decide what to do when someone drops one. Will they all stop and regroup? Give them several tries at it. Luck is the main factor here, but there are definite ways to get better at it that involve problem-solving and not just luck.

Hagoo

This is a fun activity — plain and simple. No problem-solving, no trust, no nothin' except lots of laughs. But wait, you can't laugh — that's against the rules. Oh, no!

How to Play

- Put down two lines on the floor using two ropes, tape or whatever you have around. These lines should be parallel with each other and about eight feet apart.

- Form two teams.

- Each team lines up along their line and the two teams face each other.

- The players at the right-hand end of each line step out from their lines so that they are in between the two groups.

Hagoo!

Heckling is part of the ritual, but touching is not allowed.

- These two people turn away from each other (so that their backs are towards each other).

- The groups count to 3, and these two players turn to face each other, bow deeply, and say, "Hagoo" (pronounced Hah-goooooo).

- They then walk forward, towards each other, until they meet in the middle of the two lines. Here, they look at and nod to each other and hesitate for a count of three.

- They then continue past each other and end up at opposite ends of the lines.

- They turn and face each other once again, bow, and say, "Hagoo."

Rules

1) Neither of the players can laugh or crack a smile after the first time they turn around.

2) The person who smiles or laughs first joins the opposing team. The person or person(s) who make it through without smiling stays on their original team.

3) The people standing on the sidelines can try to make the other team's player laugh. However, they cannot touch the person or step over the line.

4) The next round begins by having the two new people at the right-hand ends of the lines step out and perform the same ritual.

5) The winning team is the team with the most players when you decide to stop the game. Give each player a couple of tries.

Have You Ever...?

In his book the *Bottomless Bag*, Karl Rohnke provides a list of over five hundred *Have You Evers*. Since we use these quite often with groups, we decided to develop a list of *Have You Evers* that are more suited for younger audiences — mostly elementary to high school students. You can certainly develop more on your own. In fact, you could have developed this list but hey, we wanted to have some fun, too!

This activity is a great way to kick off a workshop or class. The questions work well with groups who have been together for years (such as a sixth grade class at the neighborhood elementary school) or a group who just met as they walked through the door for your session. They provide a fun way to show how much group members have in common. These questions provide a nice way to show that we've all done lots of different things and many of us have done some of the same things.

How to Play

A good way to do this activity is to have the group get into in a circle. Participants raise their hands or walk to a new place in the circle if their answer to the *Have You Ever* question is "yes."

Give players a few seconds to get their hands up or to move. People will often wait for someone else to respond before they do.

Things to Think About

We like to ask other questions of a few players who answered yes. Like after asking the question, *Have You Ever... walked out of a movie that you paid for?*, we might ask some of the people what movie it was. It's important to know so the rest of us don't waste money on some stupid movie. Seriously, the follow-up questions get the participants to tell a little about themselves or something they've done. But they have to do it in three words or less so you can move on to the next question and keep the game moving.

Because we hope that this book will be used by young leaders in many countries, we have tried to make our list of *Have You Evers* useful for people of various ethnic backgrounds. We encourage you to make up your own *Have You Evers* to fit your culture and audience. One important point that we'd like you to keep in mind is that the reason for doing *Have You Evers* is to allow a group to see how much they have in common through a fun, non-threatening activity. Be sure that your questions fit this description. Questions that might make certain group members feel bad should not be included. For example, "Have you ever slept on a park bench before?" is a question that some group members might answer yes to because of unfortunate family circumstances. Think about each question before using it with any group to be sure it will be fun and won't hurt anybody's feelings.

Have You Ever...

- Walked out of a movie in the middle? What movie?

- Slept through a movie that you paid for?

- Gotten an autograph from a famous person? Who?

- Broken a bone in your body? What bone?

- Hiked a mountain?

- Been out of your time zone?

- Been out of your state?

- Been out of the country?

- Tripped in front of a large group of people?

- Danced with someone you didn't like?

- Seen the President in person? Where?

- Gotten your hair cut and were embarrassed to go to school because of it?

- Seen a live python or other dangerous snake?

- Climbed up the Statue of Liberty and/or the Empire State Building?

- Traveled across the country?

- Been on TV?

- Been to a rock concert? Where? What band did you see?

- Stuck bubble gum behind your ear to store it?

- Been to the ocean?
- Known anyone who can speak 5 languages? 4? 3?
- Broken a window on your house? How or with what?
- Watched Sesame Street after the age of 10?
- Known anyone who won the lottery?
- Gotten mixed up between the boys' and girls' bathrooms and gone into the wrong one?
- Laughed loudly at a movie theater when no one else did?
- Been the only person at a movie?
- Had your stomach growl in the middle of a quiet class? In church?
- Talked on the phone with one person for six hours straight?
- Started your parents' car when you were younger than 14?
- Not been able to find the door handle when you were trying to get out of a car?
- Opened the windows of a car when the air conditioning was on?
- Had over $200 in phone bills?
- Called a 900 number?
- Turned on a radio when the volume was turned up *very* loud?
- Begged for something for a long time, and then didn't like it when you got it? What was it?
- Walked into a glass door because you didn't see it?
- Gotten a gift that you really didn't like?
- Been within 2 miles of a nuclear power plant?
- Remembered a phone number but not whose it was?
- Called a friend, but thought you were calling another?
- Eaten a whole pizza by yourself? What size?
- Broken your nose?
- Had stitches? Where?
- Fallen asleep during a class? Fireworks? A test?
- Sneezed and hiccuped at the same time?
- Played *Have You Ever* before today?

We have included some of our favorites from Karl's book, *The Bottomless Bag,* for when you are working with an adult group. Some of these may work quite well with some youth groups, just as some of ours have worked great with adult groups.

Have You Ever...

- Been in a parade?

- Eaten raw oysters?

- Broken an established school athletic record?

- Helped an animal give birth?

- Viewed an autopsy?

- Developed and printed your own black and white film?

- Swum 50 yards non-stop underwater?

- Flown in a glider?

- Eaten one of the following — tripe, cow's tongue, pig's knuckles, brain, or mountain oysters?

- Written a "letter to the editor"?

- Been stopped for speeding?

- Stayed up all night studying?

- Drank more than 10 cups of coffee in a 24-hour period?

- Stayed in a motel/hotel that cost more than $100 a night?

- Worked a night shift?

- Given blood?

- Taken a picture of your anatomy on a copying machine?

- Read a complete book by kerosene or candle light?

- Been a participant on a ropes course?

- Urinated outdoors when it was colder than zero degrees Fahrenheit?

- Totaled your car?

- Been in every state in the US (all 50)? Anyone been to 40? 30?

- Ridden in a Rolls Royce?

- Owned more than one cat at a time?

- Hitchhiked over 200 miles in one day?

- Swallowed a raw egg straight from the shell?

- Had a marriage proposal turned down?

- Tried hang-gliding?

- Had a dog lift its leg on you?

- Received a belt other than white in Karate or one of the other martial arts?

- Cut a lawn using a push mower (no engine)?

- Been in a crowd of more than 40,000 people?

- Put a bumper sticker that has a heart on it on your car ?

- Been dumped on by a seagull or other bird?

- Been accused of having an accent?

- Started a fire without matches or a lighter?

- Driven a vehicle for more than a mile in reverse?

- Played Santa Claus for a group other than family?

- Spoken to a group of more than 200 people?

- Had a blind date?

Hog Call

This activity is great with large groups.

Rumor has it that pig farmers call their pigs home by yelling, "Sooooooooie!" This game is modeled after the pig farmer's call. To get the effect that this activity is most noted for (chaos), you'll need at least twenty people. Forty-plus is best. You'll also want to be outside in a wide open field or in a big gym for this activity to be safe.

How to Play

- Have the group get into two lines facing one another. Once this has been done, have the players reach one hand out to the person across from them in order to form pairs. If there is an odd number of people in your large group, one small group can be made up of three players.

- Each pair needs to come up with two words (three for the group of three, if you have one) that are associated with each of them (for example — Black and White, Top and Bottom, Coca and Cola, etc.). Each person in the pair takes one of the two words.

- Send one line of people to one end of the field or gym and the other line to the other end. Pairs should now split up and on opposite sides of the playing area facing each other. If the two members of the pairs are lined up directly across from each other, you may want to have one line "scramble up" before proceeding with the directions.

- Have all players close their eyes and put their hands up in front of their chests (bumpers up). On "Go," the lines begin walking toward one another as players yell their partner's word, while at the same time listening for their partner, who is calling out their other word. The players continue calling their partner's words until they find each other. When they do find each other, they can open their eyes and watch the others who are still struggling to find their partners.

The Bumpers Up position helps avoid collisions.

⊕ Safety Note

If you are doing this activity in a field that has trees or other hazards or in a gym, your co-leaders need to spot the participants. If players get too close to a tree, wall or are headed in the direction of any other hazard, stop them and aim them in a safer direction.

Keep in mind that some group members will be very uncomfortable having their eyes closed, especially since they and many other people are all moving and calling out at the same time. Be sure to remind the group of Challenge By Choice and challenge them to keep their eyes closed as much as possible to fully enjoy the activity, but remind them the choice is theirs if they need to open their eyes occasionally.

(Continued)

(Safety Note, Continued)

Someone is bound to run, so before they can even think about it, be sure to mention that **running is not allowed.** Some kamikaze may not care if he runs into someone or something but others will not appreciate getting plowed over by someone else. *No running!*

Remember that the "bumpers up" position should be used any time people are blindfolded or have their eyes closed and are moving about.

Other Ideas

We frequently use *Hog Call* near the beginning or end of a workshop as a way of getting people to share goals, get to know one another or debrief the program. For example, at the beginning of a program we might have the pairs sit down for ten minutes after they have found one another and discuss a goal that they have for the day (or workshop, etc.). After the ten minutes are up, we have all of the pairs come back together as a large group and ask that players introduce their partners and the goal that they have for the Adventure experience. At the end of a program or Adventure session, *Hog Call* can be used in a similar way, except that you can have the pairs talk about their highlight of the day, what they got out of it, or whatever else would help to wrap-up your session.

Hospital Tag

This no-prop game is similar to *Everybody's It*, except that when you're tagged, you're not automatically out. Like *Everybody's It*, this game is most fun with a large group (20+), but it works just fine with smaller groups, too.

Hospital Tag can be played indoors or outside. If you are playing outside, set boundaries for the playing area — larger if you want the players to run around a lot, smaller if you want fast action.

How to Play

- Instead of having to kneel down when you get tagged, like in *Everybody's It*, this time you can be tagged three times before being out.

- Everyone starts the game with two invisible band-aids, one in each hand.

- When tagged, players need to use one of those bandaids to cover up the spot where they are tagged. They cannot remove that hand for the remainder of the game, even for three-hundredths of a second (the amount of time it takes a fourteen year-old with a three-foot, two-inch arm reach to tag someone running at 13 miles per hour at a distance of one foot, ten inches away from her — (PA Research, 1992).

- Players can still use their free hands to tag others until such time when they are tagged for a second time. Oh, no! Now the second band-aid must cover up that wound and, of course, it needs to be held in place by the player's second hand.

- Since they now have no hands left to tag people with, they just run around trying to avoid being tagged for a third time, because once that happens, that's it — they're out of band-aids and, as PA trainer Charlie Harrington is known to say, "It isn't a pretty sight."

✚ Safety Note

For safety, once players are using both hands to cover their wounds, they should not use their feet to tag other players. The only exception to this is an older youth or an adult group that you trust will tag in a safe way and without tripping other players.

Human Knot

This classic activity is usually known by people of all ages when you present it. But knowing it doesn't make it any easier, because the knot turns out different every time. *Human Knot* is great for indoors or outdoors and requires no props, so it's easy to fit it into all kinds of programs.

How to Play

- Have the group get into a circle.

- First, have the players put their left hands into the center of the circle.

- Next, have everyone grab the left hand of someone else in the circle.

If a player looks like he is in an uncomfortable position, let him break to reposition himself.

- Now have players put their right hands into the circle and have them join right hands with someone else. Make sure that no one is holding both the left and right hands of the same person (otherwise they'll have their own two-person circle).

- Now the group has to untangle itself, without breaking hands, so that when they're done they are in one large circle.

Things to Think About

Depending on how the group's hands were joined at the beginning they may not always end up in a circle. At times they may be in more than one circle or still in a knot. If the group has been at it for a long time and it looks like they have knotted themselves up real good, you can give them one free hand break. What this means is that you can have two people break their hand grip. The group will now try to form a straight line when they untangle.

Good luck and, yes, it can be done!

⊕ Safety Note

> Only one person can move at a time. If a player's arm is being twisted, have him let go of the other player's hand for a second to reposition himself in a more comfortable way and then rejoin with the other person (don't let them untangle any knots in the process, though!).

Human Treasure Hunt

This activity is a great way for people to meet other people and see what they (even complete strangers) have in common.

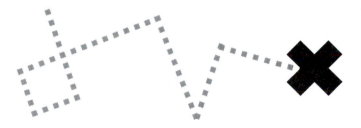

How to Play

- Every player receives a list.

- A time limit (usually 15 to 20 minutes) is set by the leader.

- The players try to find other people who fit the statements on their lists.

- When a player finds someone who fits a category, they have that player sign their name next to the statement. **Each player can sign someone else's paper just once.** This prevents players from meeting just one person who they have a lot in common with and instead requires them to mingle and meet many people.

- By the end of the time limit, each player wants to get as many signatures possible. Can anyone get signatures for every statement?

Other Ideas

The statements can be changed to fit age group, location, and/or interests of the members.

Human Treasure Hunt

_____ is born in the same month as you

_____ can speak a foreign language

_____ has been on TV, radio or in the news (why:)

_____ has performed on stage anywhere

_____ has been elected to a position

_____ volunteers for an organization or cause

_____ has been in a parade (why:)

_____ has a unique skill or talent

_____ has the same number of siblings as you

_____ wrote a letter to the editor (why:)

_____ has traveled outside the U.S.A. (where:)

_____ established a record

_____ can play a musical instrument

_____ climbed a mountain over 10,000 feet

_____ has lived outside the U.S.A. for more than a year

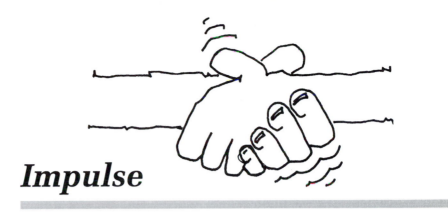

Impulse

This activity is a good one to use early on in a session because it is so simple. It also allows you to introduce goal-setting. *Impulse* usually works best with groups of fewer than thirty players. If the group gets too large, action gets slow and people can get bored.

How to Play

- Get the group in a circle and have everyone hold hands with the people beside them. Choose a starting person.

- Have the starter squeeze one of the hands she is holding and have that person (the one who received the squeeze) squeeze the hand of the next person and so on. This hand squeezing continues so that the *Impulse* goes around the circle until it gets back to the player who started it.

Other Ideas

- Have the group pick a goal for the amount of time it might take for the impulse to go around the circle. Try to help them find a goal that everyone can agree on.

- Try sending the *Impulse* in a different direction from the first time you went around.

- Have the group try it with their eyes closed — is it any harder or slower?

- Try it with a new starting player.

- Try sending an *Impulse* in both directions at the same time by having the starter squeeze both hands at the same time. The impulse will cross somewhere near the halfway point of the circle and both impulses should get back to the starter (should is a key word here!!!). Give the group a few tries if they lose an *Impulse* somewhere along the way.

Knee Slap

The staff at Project Adventure learned this activity from some Russian college students a few years ago and it has been used with all kinds of groups ever since. We like to introduce it as the "rocket scientist" version of *Impulse*, because it adds a new level of complexity.

How to Play

- Have your group sit cross legged in a circle on the floor.

- Players put their hands on the knees of the people on either side of them. Each person's left hand should be on the right knee of the person on their left. Each person's right hand should be on the left leg of the person to their right. If they can't figure this out, we recommend playing something simpler instead, like "go fish." But seriously, be sure you've done this one yourself first so that you can understand how to help them get set up.

- Like in other versions of *Impulse,* you need a starting person. (How about the person whose birthday is closest to today?)

- This starting person decides which way the impulse will go and which of her hands she will start with.

- Starting with that hand, the impulse of *gentle* knee slaps must go in the order of hands. So, if the starter begins with her right hand, the next to go will be the person to her right, whose left knee she has her right hand on. Guess you better look at the photo.

- A good goal at first is to see if the group can get all the way around the circle without a mistake.

- If the group can do that, they may want to speed it up and try to beat a time goal.

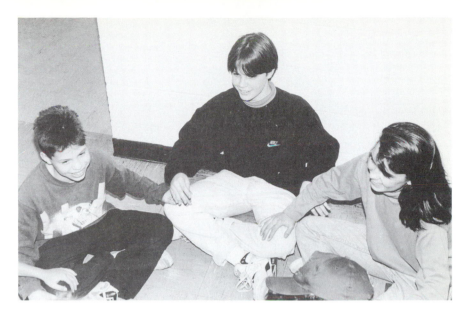

Other Ideas

A nice way to end a day of activities is to have the players stand up and put their hands on the shoulders of their neighbors. The activity is the same as above except that players tap their neighbor on the shoulder instead of the knee. Hands still need to go in order. As the players tap their neighbors, have them say, "Good job" to that person. It's a real nice celebration of a great day of group fun and achievement.

Things to Think About

Recent studies conducted by the authors of this book have found that 46% of all groups have at least one member who ends up yelling at his or her own hand to, "Get going!" As the time pressures of a goal cause a temporary shutdown of all brain functions, confusion of which hand belongs to who gets greater. In the quest for a "Knee Slap World Record," it is quite common for a person to be yelling "get going" at his own hand because he thinks that the hand belongs to someone else. As soon as he notices that this hand wears the same watch and that the sleeves of its shirt are identical to the material of his shirt, something clicks in, and he realizes that it is his own hand that he is yelling at!

Line-Up

This activity is a great way to mix people up in order to create teams or groups for other activities. It's also great fun on its own, too.

How to Play

- Tell the group that from this second on there is to be no talking. If they listen to you and don't talk, call us and we'll send you a prize, because it's never worked for us!

- Anyway, the reason that you don't want them to talk is because their job is to line themselves up in order by month and day of their birthdays (not year). Of course, *they must do this without talking or lip syncing* (you know — moving your mouth like Milli Vanilli).

- Tell the players that you'd like them to shoot for no errors — everyone would be lined up in the right place. If you get a bunch of blank stares when you give these directions, you could give an example like this: if Steve's birthday is June 12th, Sam's is February 10th, Jennifer's is November 23rd and Sean's is August 25th, then we would need to line up as Sam, Steve, Sean and Jennifer.

Things to Think About

Based on experience, here are a few things you might expect to happen and some of the ways that we have dealt with them:

- Which end is January and which end is December? Our response is usually a shrug of the shoulders. (Let them figure it out.)

- People that shy away from failure or get frustrated easily will start talking even though you've said not to. We like to say something like, "We know that you can do it by talking, but that's not much of a challenge. Look around to see how other players are communicating without talking."

- Try to be sure that there are no pencils, pens or other writing instruments around the room. Although writing their birthdays on their hands or the wall or somewhere else is certainly a creative solution, it is also an easy way out. This activity challenges groups to communicate in ways that we are not used to — ways other than writing or talking.

- The large group might break off into smaller groups. This is fine to begin with (if you've got a large group it's actually a much easier way to begin solving the problem), but you may want to remind them periodically that you need one long line at the end.

Give the group as much time as it takes for everyone to get situated. We like to ask the entire group if they think that everyone is in the right spot. This puts the responsibility of getting people to the right place on the entire group. By doing this, if one person ends up in the wrong place, the other players can't get on this person's case. It was *everyone's* responsibility to solve the problem together. If the group does think that they are in the

right order, you would ask which end of the line is the earliest part of the year. Starting with the first person at that end of the line, walk down the line and have players yell their birth date when you get to them. If you come across someone who is in the wrong spot, have them move to the correct place.

How did they do? In a group of thirty or more people, three or less errors is very good. For a group less that thirty, under three is impressive. We've had a few groups do it with no errors.

Other Ideas

- With adult groups, like your teachers at school, you can have them line up by years of experience at their job instead of birthdays.

- As we mentioned, you can use this activity to divide a group into teams or pairs. If your next activity involves people being paired up and you want to do this in a more creative way than asking them to find a partner, you can have them do *Line-Up*. After you've checked to see how they did with the activity, you can have them fold the line in half so that each person is standing across from another person. Start this by having the person on one end of the line walk to the person on the other end of the line. Others should follow his or her lead until everyone is standing across from another person and, viola!, you have pairs. If you have an odd number of people you can either join in or have one group of three — whatever makes more sense for the next activity you have in mind.

- If your next activity involves small groups, have people count off by the number of groups you'd like to have. For example, if you want four groups of eight for the next activity, start at one end of the line with the first person being number One, the second person a Two, then a Three, and a Four. Rather than a Five, the person after Four becomes another One. We have used this method to divide up groups for Dialogue Nights (See Page 178) so that we had a good mix of youths and adults at each table.

Link-Up Tag

Link-Up Tag seems to be liked by people of all ages. It is a good "early" activity because it gets people moving around and having fun together. It is also an excellent activity for a medium to large-sized group.

How to Play

- Set up boundaries for a playing area (keep it pretty tight).
- Have everyone in the group find a partner.
- Have each player hook elbows with his or her partner.
- Choose one pair to begin the game.
- Of these two people, have one person be *it* (the chaser), the other then becomes the *chasee*.

- The other pairs remain stationary throughout the game and the players put their outside hands on their hips and stick their elbows out.

- The chasee wants to avoid being tagged by the person who is *it*. The way that the chasee can get to safety is to *Link Up* with another pair by linking arms with one of them.

- When the chassee links on to another pair, the person on the opposite side of this pair must now release because there cannot be three people in a pair. This person is now the chasee and can only avoid becoming *it* by linking up somewhere else, and so on, and so on.

- If the chasee is tagged before linking up, he or she becomes it. This person needs to spin around once to give the old *it* a chance to get away and/or link up.

- The game ends when you, as the leader, call it to a stop (maybe five to ten minutes).

Another Idea

For more of a challenge, the pairs can wander throughout the designated playing area. We normally don't add this part for a while so that everyone gets a chance to understand the original rules first.

✚ Safety Note

Play this game at a fast walk (NO RUNNING). When tagging, be sure people are gentle — no pushing or shoving. And be sure people are keeping their elbows to themselves. Keep the pairs stationary until you are confident that these other safety issues are being followed. Adding movement of the pairs increases the chance of someone tripping, so we recommend that you wait five minutes or more before adding this step. If it looks safe early on, this new step should be plenty safe, too.

Miss Mumble!

This is a good small-group activity that is done simply for laughs. The only problem is that, like *Hagoo*, laughing is not allowed! If you have a large group, you may want to split players up into smaller groups of 6–8. We use this story to set an appropriately serious mood for the players.

This is the ancient ritual of the African Notooths. The leader of the tribe is missing. Every evening the people of the tribe meet together. They meet in a circle around a ritual fire, and ask each other if they have seen Miss Mumble! Now remember, nobody laughs in the tribe because it is such a serious thing that Miss Mumble is missing.

How to Play

- Get the players to form a circle. Pick a player to start and have this player turn to the person on the right and say, "Have you seen Miss Mumble?" This must be done without smiling or showing any teeth.

- The person who is asked the question then says in reply, "No. Let me ask my neighbor."

- This player then turns to her right and says, again without smiling or showing her teeth, "Have you seen Miss Mumble?"

- When anyone in the circle shows their teeth or smiles they are out of the game — but only until everyone is out and then you can start again.

- NOTE: Players can say other things besides the set question and reply to make others laugh.

Moonball

Moonball is another old standby because of its 100% guaranteed fun-factor. It works well with people of all ages and with any size group. It can be played indoors or outdoors, just as long as you have a pretty large playing area, like a gym.

Things You'll Need

One or more beach balls

How to Play

Explain to the players that their objective is to see how many times they can hit the ball into the air without letting it hit the ground. Once the ball hits the ground the count starts again at zero. The only other rules are that the beach ball must be hit with hands only (see variations) and that it can't be hit by the same person two times in a row.

Things to Think About

This is another activity where goal setting can be talked about and tried. You may want to give the group a trial run to see how well they do. Once they have done this, you can have them establish a group goal, like how many hits they think they'll get before the ball hits the ground. Give them several attempts to reach this goal and once they have made it, see if they'd like to go for more.

Many times, right after the ball hits the ground, someone will pick it up and hit it to start a new attempt. If this is happening over and over again, you may want to step in and give them a two-minute time-out for planning. We have seen many unique strategies for getting a high number of hits. Give the group time to plan some new strategies. During a debrief (at the end of the activity or end of the day), you can ask them if they stopped to think things through. Players often admit that they get caught up in working *harder* when working *smarter* was what was actually needed. A good lesson for life.

Sometimes on a windy day, the group will blame the wind for their difficulties in getting a "good" number of hits. Usually, the group has not factored the wind into their strategy. They may be set up in a circle and the ball keeps blowing out of the circle. The real problem is not the wind, it's the fact that they have not put people downwind to get the ball when the wind blows.

Other Ideas

After a few tries you can begin adding two points for a *header* — hitting the ball with your head instead of your hands. You'll soon see why it is worth two points — it is much more difficult to control.

Sometimes with a group of more than thirty people, not everyone involves themselves, or a few people come up with a strategy that involves just a few of them. One way to get everyone involved in the fun and cooperation is to use more than one Moonball. Have the group keep track of the hits of both balls and add the numbers together once both have hit the ground to get the group score.

Steve recently found a neat new toy to use during Moonball. It is called Balzac. Balzac is a balloon cover — simply put a balloon (and water or coins) in the Balzac and blow up the balloon. You now have a ball that resembles a beach ball. If you've put water in the balloon or coins in the Balzac it will fly in all kinds of weird directions. Check out your local toy store for a Balzac.

⊕ Safety Note

> Some leaders allow feet to be used. We prefer not to because a high kicking foot becomes a real safety problem for other players.

robinjessicarogersanuabebarbiezachsusansteve

better known as

(Name Impulse)

This is a fun indoor or outdoor game that requires no props and allows a group to work on names, goal setting and problem-solving.

The object of this form of *Impulse* (See Page 115) is to pass each player's name around the circle as fast as possible.

How to Play

- Gather the group in a circle.

- Ask for a volunteer to start the activity.

- Ask this player which way she would like the impulse to go (left or right, not both ways at once).

- To start the activity have this person say her name.

- As soon as the starter has said her name, the next person (in the direction the starter chooses) will say his name.

- This continues around the circle with players saying their own names as soon as the players beside them have said theirs.

- Time how long it takes for the *Name Impulse* to get all the way around the circle and back to the starter.

- See if the players think they can do it any faster. If they do, give them one minute to figure out how they are going to improve upon the time they just got.

- Let them do the attempt/plan cycle a few times.

Things to Think About

We're always asked what's *legal* and what's not during this activity. Common questions include:

- Can we use nicknames if they're shorter than our real name?

- Can we abbreviate our names (say S instead of Susan)?

- Can I tap the next person when I'm saying my name?

- Can we each drink five cups of coffee before we try it?

Our usual answers are: yes, yes, yes, no. The first three ideas are the result of good ol' creative thinking. The last is not allowed by the International Olympic Committee (IOC) so why should we allow it? After all, this activity is at least as important as the Olympics!

Pairs Tag

Pairs Tag is a quick introductory activity for people of all ages. Adults especially like this one! Like other tag games, any size group will work, but the more the merrier. It works indoors and outdoors, but you will need enough room for everyone to move around in, plus a little extra.

Pairs Tag works well even indoors. But remember— Bumpers Up, and no running!

How to Play

- Have everybody find a partner.

- Explain to the players that they will be playing tag with just their partners.

- Ask each pair to choose one player to be *it*. These players then chase their own partners at a fast walk (NO RUNNING!).

- When the players who are *it* tag their partners, the players who just got tagged spin around three times before going after their partner who just tagged them.

- A fairly tight playing area works great for this activity. A classroom with desks pushed to the side even works well for a school class. We've led this activity with over one-hundred people using only half of a basketball court.

- The game ends when you, as the leader, decide to end it. (Just three minutes will usually work up a good sweat!)

✚ Safety Note

As with all of the activities in the book, be sure to tell the group that when you yell "Stop," they must stop. Have players walk (remind them "NO RUNNING") with bumpers up — hands up in front so that contact with others will be with hands and not foreheads.

Peek-A-Who

Peek-A-Who is a high-energy, hootin' and hollerin', name game. It is best done with groups of fifteen to twenty five — this keep the players moving and everyone involved.

Things You'll Need

A blanket, couch cover, official PA "Peek-A-Who" screen or very large piece of fabric. Whichever you choose, make sure it is not *see-through*.

How to Play

- Divide the group in half. Have two people (you and another leader or a volunteer) hold up the blanket. Put half of the group on one side of the blanket and half on the other side. Make sure everyone is sitting two or three feet back from the blanket, and be sure that nobody can see anyone on the other side.

- Each team chooses one person to go forward to the blanket. These players should face the screen and be very close to it. Choosing this person *silently* is best, but let the players discover this after they've blurted out, "Hey Zach, you go up there," a few times. It won't take them long to figure out that this makes it pretty easy for the other team.

- On the count of three, the people holding the blanket drop it to the ground and the two chosen players, who are now facing each other nose-to-nose, try to correctly name the person across from them. They can receive no help from their teammates — it's one-on-one!

- Whoever names their opponent first *wins* that person for their team.

- The first team to have everyone on it is the winning team. With larger groups this may never happen, so you may want to set a time limit at the beginning and then whichever team has the most people wins.

Things to Think About

Remind the group not to get *too* competitive — you're only trying to learn people's names and have some fun! It's the slightly competitive nature of this game that makes it fun. But be prepared to have people challenge your refereeing with statements like, "No... I said Barbi before she said my name!" In this case just reach into your pocket, fake like you pulled something out and pretend that you are watching a very small TV monitor. After a second or two tell the groups that after reviewing the super-dooper-slow-mo, you are sticking with your decision. If you know the people you could also say, "Lighten up, Frances." If you've never seen the movie *Stripes*, stop reading right now and march down to your local video store.

Other Ideas

For groups that know each other fairly well, an addition that is a bit more challenging for everyone goes like this:

- Have the two chosen people sit with their backs to the blanket. This time, when the blanket drops, they cannot see each other and the only way of guessing the other person's name is by using the information that their teammates provide (but they can't say the person's name!). My teammates might tell me that the person is a male, in twelfth grade, with a beard and a pierced ear. "That's Abe!"

- This new rule challenges a group to use information other than just looks to identify each other. Something worth mentioning to the group is that you want them to use positive descriptions of each other. Remind the group of the Full Value Contract — respecting and valuing each other and no put-downs.

- With a group or class that has people of different races, nationalities, physical abilities or other diversity, this activity allows these differences to be viewed in a positive way, as part of who we are. This is why it is critical that you say positive things about the person. We can start feeling good about our racial, physical and gender differences when we are allowed to use them as positive information about a person. For example, if I were playing with the group of my co-authors, my team might say that the person that is across from me is Nepalese. I know that this must be Sanu. My group used information about who she is with full respect for the fact that her ethnic background is obviously an important part of who she is. To tell me it is someone with black hair, a female and in eighth grade also describes Jessica. The piece of information that helps me to know that it is Sanu and not Jessica is her heritage. We are sometimes taught to not talk about these differences. We think that we should celebrate them.

A Story

This activity is one of our favorites, because people from kindergarten to the elderly seem to always love it! Here's one of Steve's favorite *Peek-A-Who* stories:

A few years ago I was doing a workshop with some students from the Townshend (VT) area Leadership Project Team. We were conducting a games day for the elementary school in Putney, and we pulled out our blanket for another fun game of *Peek-A-Who*.

Late in the game, two of the younger students (probably first or second graders) came up to the two sides of the blanket. The two youth leaders dropped the blanket and the two students just stared at each other's faces with jaws wide open. After thirty seconds of staring at each other and not coming up with any guesses, the leaders sent the two back to their teams. Now the funny part — both kids were wearing sweatshirts with their first names painted across the top. If either one had looked down from the other's face, they would have been able to just read the name off the sweatshirt, but in the heat of battle they just froze!

People to People

A fun way to wrap up a day, *People to People* sometimes works best at the end of a session because it involves physical contact, which many people are at first uncomfortable with. The group will get more comfortable with each other throughout your Adventure program, which will make *People to People* a more fun and positive experience.

How to Play

- Start this game by getting your group in a circle. If you don't have an even number of people for this game, you should participate to make it even.

- Have the players begin snapping their fingers to create a rhythm. While they're warming up tell, them that any time you say a body part they must find someone else to join up with using this body part. Each time a new body part is called out, pairs need to split up so that players are with different partners each time.

- Start out by singing *People to People* a few times — a nice bluesy sound works well, although an opera version may generate some strange looks.

Knee to Knee...

Shoulder to shoulder…

- After singing *People to People* a few times, name a body part, like hand, by saying, "Hand to Hand!"

- Next say, "People to People" and point to someone in the group and tell her to name another body part. Other examples would be "Head to Head" or "Elbow to Elbow."

- Continue with this for five to ten body parts.

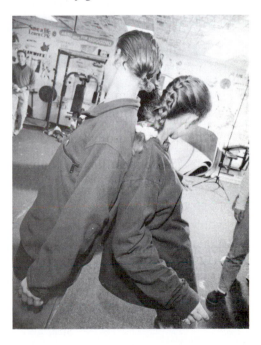

Back to back…

Popsicle Push-Up

This is a quick, team-building, muscle-flexing, brain-teasing, just fun activity.

How to Play

- Break up your large group into smaller groups of four players each.

- Set each group up so that they look like the photo at right.

- The object of the activity is for the groups of four to do a push-up.

- The only rule is that all four people must do the push-up together, so that all players' bodies are entirely off the ground except for their hands.

- See if a group can hold the push-up for a count of three.

Things to Think About

Like many Project Adventure activities there are some ways to solve this problem that involve more than just strength. People of various sizes should be able to do this activity together if they put their brains *and* muscles into it. One way that we have seen groups figure this out is to have the lighter group members start doing their push-up half a second before the others. This way, they are part way up before they receive the

Puuuush!

weight of the other person on their back. Encourage the group to try to figure out creative solutions by asking questions like, "How can you do this by using brain power instead of just muscle power?"

Your leadership can be helpful to mix up groups differently than they might do on their own. You could let the players make their own groups for the first try and then encourage them to join up with other people to try again. Help them make male-female mixes and groups with people of various physical abilities. When groups like this succeed at the activity, it is especially rewarding.

Potential Problem Pit

This is a good two-person, trust-building activity. It is also an activity that gets people talking about their reactions and feelings and so requires some debriefing.

Things You'll Need

Rope

Lots and lots of objects — squeaky toys, balls, rubber insects, balloons — anything that won't hurt or be hurt if stepped on, but the more unusual and funny the better.

Blindfolds

How to Play

- Before you start, use the rope to form a rectangular area for a group of 20 people — an area about 8 feet by 25 feet works well. Inside this area place your collection of objects, leaving enough space in between them to place a foot or two.

- Split the players into pairs

- One partner is blindfolded and led to one end of the *Pit*.

- The un-blindfolded partners leave their partners and step to the sides. It is their responsibility to guide the blindfolded partner through the *Pit* without stepping on any of the objects. They are not allowed to physically touch the blindfolded partners — only to talk to them.

- Keep track of each time the blindfolded partners touch an object with their foot. Before starting, you can have each pair make a goal of how many touches they will allow themselves.

- After players get through, have them switch with their partners so that all players take a turn going through the *Pit*.

Other Ideas

The *Pit* could be considered as symbolic of life, and before starting players write on a blown-up balloon one despair they have of life. They then place that balloon somewhere in the *Pit*. The partners who are blindfolded must be guided to their balloons and pick them up and carry them out of the *Pit* with them. When all participants have made it through the *Pit*, all of the despairs can then be destroyed.

Quail Shooter's Delight

Looking for a less active, yet very fun, activity? Here's one that your group should enjoy. It's a good rainy day activity, since it can be done indoors as well as outside.

There is a rumor among hunters that the best way to shoot a quail is to keep your eye on one and hope that you get that one. We hear that quails usually fly in groups, and if you focus on the whole group, you may come up empty-handed. That same idea might be helpful in this game — hence the name *Quail Shooter's Delight.*

Things You'll Need

Lots of soft, throwable objects like softies, rubber chickens, nerf balls, fleece balls (one per group member)

How to Play

- Get the group in a circle.

- Ask for a volunteer to go into the middle of the circle. This person is going to be the "hunter."

- Give each person in the circle one of the soft objects. These will be the *quails*.

- The hunter counts, "one, two, three, throw," and all the players loft their quails high into the air and toward the hunter.

- The hunter tries to catch as many quails as possible. You can keep track of "world records" if you want to make it competitive. Catching three is incredible. Zero or one are more common.

- Give everyone a chance to take a turn in the middle.

Things to Think About

If you have a large group or want a different way of playing this, more than one person can go in the middle. The throwers do the same thing as before and the score is the total number of balls caught by the hunters.

Quick Line-Up

Quick Line-Up is a very fun, action-oriented, large group, team-building activity. You'll want to be in a gym, large room or field for this one because of the fast action.

This game works best with large groups — like 30 to 200!

How to Play

- The leader has the group form a square with an equal number of people on each of the four sides (or as close to an equal number as possible). Players should be standing shoulder-to-shoulder (but not smushed!) and facing the inside of the square. The leader is in the middle and is facing one of the four sides of the square.

- Each side of the square represents a team, therefore there are four teams.

Be sure that you are facing one of the teams straight on.

- For the first part of the activity, all players in the square need to remember who is on their right and who is on their left (the end players only have to remember the person next to them who is on their team, they don't need to worry about the person on the other team). Give the

Quick Line-Up!

group ten seconds to check out who is beside them — if it's a group whose members don't know each other well, give them a minute and have players introduce themselves to their teammates.

- The *teams* must also remember how they are lined up in relation to the leader who is in the middle of the square. As the leader you want to make it very obvious which way you are facing — no angles or anything, just straight on so that one team is directly in front of you, one is on your left, one on your right and one team is directly behind you.

- Now that you are all set up, the game goes like this: You (the leader) spin around in the middle of the square and stop, facing a new direction. When you stop, yell, "Quick Line-Up!"

- Each team must now line up on the same side of you that they began on. For example, the team that started behind you has to be behind you again; the team that started on your left has to be directly on your left; etc.

- Not only does each team have to line up in relation to you, but the players on each team must also be lined up in the same exact order as they were to begin with — that's why you had them remember who was on their right and left.

- When a group is in the right place, and all of its team members are lined up in the right order, they need to join hands and yell, "Quick Line-Up" while lifting their hands into the air.

- The first team to do this is without a doubt the *World Quick Line-Up Champions*. But before they even have time to do their *Sports Illustrated* interview, twirl around, stop facing a new direction and yell, "Quick Line-Up" to begin another round.

Things to Think About

Forget trying to referee this game. I don't think we've ever had a group get all its members in place before yelling, "Quick Line-Up." Rather than allow arguments to develop about which team was first to line up, just twirl around and yell, "Quick Line-Up" to start the chaos all over again! We'll usually do ten rounds or so.

✛ Safety Note

> This is an activity that can go from great fun to no fun in the matter of a millisecond if someone gets hurt. Recognizing this, you should keep the following safety considerations at the forefront of your mind:
>
> If the group you're working with seems too wound up, skip Quick Line-Up until another day;
>
> With younger groups (sixth grade or below) or a group that you aren't sure buys into the "safety first" motto, have a "no running" rule;
>
> A common strategy that a team will develop is holding hands so that they all move together. We usually allow this unless they are running over other people on the way to their new spot;
>
> As always, the safety of everyone in the group is shared between you and the group. If you feel an accident is possible because of the way anyone or group is acting, you need to either talk with them about it right then or stop the activity.

Rainmaker

Rainmaker is a powerful closing activity because of the beautiful sound the group makes doing it. A group of twenty or more will make the best sounds, fewer than ten probably would not work too well.

Something special always happens when members of a group all work together on a task. But did you know that a group can actually make it rain, no matter what the weather? Ah yes, the power of a group!

How to Play

- Get everyone in a circle and sitting on the floor or ground.

- You, the leader, get in the middle of the circle and either sit or stand.

- Explain to the players that *when you look at them* they will begin doing the motion that you are doing and that they will keep doing this motion until you come back to each of them with a new one. Also encourage players to keep quiet during the activity. Any noises that are not part of the activity will take away from the fun of it.

- Begin the activity by looking at one player in the circle. While looking at this person, start rubbing your hands together. About every second or two, look to the next person in the circle while continuing to rub your hands together. This will send the hand-rubbing around the circle one person at a time. When you get back to the first player, everyone in the group should be rubbing their hands together. This will sound like soft rain.

- Starting with that first person again, begin sending around the second sound — snapping your fingers with both hands. The other players should keep rubbing their hands together and only start snapping their fingers when you get to them. Again, go in order around the circle initiating this sound with each player in turn. This will sound like heavy rain drops hitting the ground.

- When you get back to the first player again, start hitting your thighs with the palms of your hands. Follow the same pattern around the circle. Again, everyone should keep doing the finger snap until you look at them to do the thigh slap.

- The next sound is hitting the floor with the palms of your hands. As more and more people in the circle get doing this it will sound like a torrential downpour.

- When you get back to the first person after the floor slapping, start doing the whole process backward to make it sound like the storm is slowly ending. Have the first person go back to the thigh slapping, pass that around, then the finger-snapping, then the rubbing of hands.

- When you get back to the first player, after everyone is rubbing their hands, just go around looking at people with your hands doing nothing. By doing this, fewer and fewer people will be doing the hand-rubbing, making it sound like the last moments of a storm before the sun comes up.

Beautiful, huh?

Speed Rabbit

This activity is just plain old fun. *Speed Rabbit* works best a few games into a session because people are asked to get just a little bit goofy. It may seem like a kids' game (which it is) but it is an adult favorite, as well. To be sure everyone is involved, groups of 8 to 15 work best, but see *Other Ideas* for using it with larger groups. You will need a large open space and a group of people who want to have a wicked awesome time.

How to Play

Rabbit!

- Have your group form a circle.

- Choose one person to be in the center of the circle — to keep it simple, we'll call this person the leader.

- Have the leader turn around and around, and randomly stop and point to someone and call out a character. (See photos for some characters that can be created.)

- The player who is pointed to is the main body of the character, and the people that are on each side of this player are the two sides.

- The leader counts to ten, fast or slow, and if the three people creating the character haven't completed it by the time the leader reaches ten, the person pointed to (the *body*) replaces the leader in the center of the circle. The old leader re-enters the circle with the other players.

- Start by demonstrating the different characters that you will use during the activity. We usually start with three choices and might add a fourth or fifth later on in the game if the group is really into the activity.

Elephant!

Other Ideas

If you have a large group, try two players in the center of the circle both pointing and calling out characters.

The game ends whenever you feel like the group is starting to lose interest or when you want to move on to another activity. A fun way to end the game is to have leaders stay in the center when people goof up or don't get done quickly enough. Since the person pointed to comes into the circle when this happens there will now be two leaders in the middle who can call on any unsuspecting trio. As players make mistakes, they come into the middle, but the old ones stay there, too. By doing this, the number of people in the middle grows and grows until there's no one left outside. It is at precisely this time that you ask the group to join together in reciting the Preamble to the Constitution (or the first page of Dr. Seuss' *Cat in the Hat*, if they wish).

Feel free to make up any new characters (we made up most of these!).

Palm Tree!

Striker

This is a great fast-action, large group, indoor/outdoor game that looks like a cross between soccer and basketball.

Things You'll Need

A large inflated beach ball, or two or three

How to Play

- Split the group into two even teams.

- A goal line for each team should be marked off using cones or other markers. The size of the goals and distance between them is up to you, taking into consideration the group's size, age and ability.

- The object is for each team to try to score goals against the other.

Rules

1) The game is started by having a member from each team jump for the ball at center court — like a basketball jump-ball.

2) The ball is passed down the field/gym by the team members, each team heading towards the other team's goal line.

3) No intentional body contact is allowed and striking the ball can only be done with a flat palm (it makes a real satisfying sound that way).

4) Points are earned each time one team gets the ball over the other team's goal.

5) After a goal has been scored, the team that has just scored on gets the ball and starts off from their own goal.

Things to Think About

This is a very active game with no penalties or time-outs, so the game should be ended when you see that the group is starting to get tired. By stopping a game before people get too tired, you can help avoid a lot of accidents.

With a group of more than 20 people, another ball can be added.

Texas Big-Foot

This is a good end-of-the-day activity because it brings everyone together (and we mean together!). It is most fun with groups larger than 15. There are no success or failure, problem-solving or communication challenges — just good group fun!

How to Play

One, Two, Three, Step!

- Get your group into a circle (leaders, too) so that the players' arms are around the shoulders of their neighbors.

- Tell the group that you will be asking them to take a series of giant steps in toward the center of the circle — on your commands only. Since, as the saying goes, "Everything is BIG in Texas," player's steps need to be as *BIG* as they can make them.

- For the first step, have all the players lift their left legs nice and high (have them hold it there for a second or two) and then count "One, two, three, STEP!" Have everyone hold their left foot in that place for a few seconds and then do the second step.

- You've probably figured this out by now, but just in case, the second step would be a BIG step with the right foot.

- The group will be getting mighty squished (a highly scientific term meaning that they are smooshed) together by now.

- Even though there's little to no space left in the middle of the circle, give the group one last, "One, two, three, STEP!" for good measure (and good fun!).

✚ Safety Note

> You never know what physical limitations or injuries people may have so be sure to do two things before you start: Remind players of the Full Value Contract — that, "We're going to take care of each other" — to prevent any over-zealousness. Take a second or two between steps and give players time to let their neighbors know if their arms are in an awkward position, their foot is being stepped on, or they are in some other uncomfortable position.

Toe Tag

This fun, fast-action game is not for every group. Use your judgment on whether or not to use it based on the concern for safety that the group has shown in other activities.

Things You'll Need

Feet, toes and shoes are all that are needed, but people may want to bring along the rest of their bodies just for the heck of it.

How to Play

- Divide the group into pairs.

- Have each pair find a sizable spot to call their own. They'll probably be moving around a lot.

- The object of the activity is for the players to use their feet to tag (step *lightly* on) their partner's feet. Players who tag their partner's feet first are the winners.

- Start the activity by having the partners stand back-to-back.

- On your state signal they turn around and go at it.

➕ Safety Note

> This activity has the potential to get out of hand if someone is not taking the safety issue seriously. Stomping on another player's feet is not allowed, nor is kicking people in the shins. If you see any of this going on, you've got to stop those players, or the activity immediately.

Toss-A-Name Game

This activity has got to be one of the most popular and often used by Adventure leaders around the world. It's also a great way of helping people in new groups learn each others' names. Both you and the players in your group will be truly amazed at how quickly names can be remembered using *Toss-A-Name Game*.

Things You'll Need

Soft objects, like fleece balls

How to Play

- Get the group in a circle.

- The leader starts by holding an object (nerf ball, fleece ball, rubber chicken or some other soft object) and saying his name. The leader then passes the object to the player next to him and he says his name. As players receive the object in turn, they say their names. Have a couple of go-rounds like this (maybe once one way then switch directions and go back the other way). Now you're ready for the next part.

- Toss the object around the circle in random order by calling a player's name (make sure they have eye contact with you before you throw the object) and then tossing it underhanded to that player. The receiver continues the game by calling someone else's name and tossing to them. The game should go until everyone has gotten the object at least a couple of times. The leader can speak up at some point during the game to see if everyone has received the object. If not, have the person with the object toss it to one of the players who hasn't received it until everyone has been included.

- After doing this for a while, ask the group members now to thank the person who tossed the object to them by name; i.e., "Thank you, Abe." Keep calling the person's name who you're throwing to as well. This step challenges players to learn more names because they could get the ball tossed to them by someone in the group whose name they don't know yet. In which case they say,"Thank you… ?"

- The leader can add more objects to the group after step two. Be sure players know that they keep the same rules as before and that the only difference is the number of objects being tossed among the players.

✚ Safety Note

> Because the noise level always increases with more objects being added, before starting this part remind people to call the name of the person that they will throw to and to be sure that this person is looking before throwing.

Other Ideas

At the end of the game, the leader can ask for a volunteer to name all of the people in the group. If no one volunteers to name all of the people, ask for a volunteer who thinks they can name 3/4 of the group. An added challenge: the leader can ask people in the group to change places in the circle and stand beside different people than before. Now ask for volunteers to name everyone in the circle. This is a bit more difficult because we sometimes remember a name because of where someone was standing ("OK, Robin is beside Sanu") and not because of what they look like.

Traffic Jam

Got a superior, high-functioning, outstanding group that needs a *tough* challenge? *Traffic Jam* is the answer. Because it is a toughie, you might want to consider putting it later on in your sequence of activities. This will let the group practice their problem-solving skills before being faced with a major challenge. *Traffic Jam* can be done outdoors or inside. You will need to divide your group into smaller groups of eight to do it. If you have some people left over, they can serve as part of the problem-solving team of another group.

Yes, it can be done!

How to Play

- Lay out nine pieces of paper on the floor that have the following designs: The pieces should be about two feet apart.

- Each of the eight people should stand on one of the pieces of paper with an arrow on it. They should face in the direction that the arrow is pointing.

- The object of the activity is to get the groups to switch sides. (The group on the left side is trying to get to the right side and those on the right to the left). The players need to be in the same order when they get to the other side.

Hmmmmmm...

Rules

1) People must face the same way the whole time.

2) No one can pass someone facing the same way as them (someone whose back is toward them).

3) A person can only go around one person at a time.

4) A person must have an empty spot to stand on when they go around a person.

5) No one can ever move backward.

6) Only one person can move at a time.

Things to Think About

You need to be aware that some groups will not solve this problem in the time you have or they may get frustrated to the point of wanting to stop. Neither of these situations are bad, just be prepared to process with the group what did happen (both positive and negative). Encourage them to keep thinking about it or try to solve it on paper so that they can try again next time if they'd like. Most likely, they are very close to the solution and, after a little time away from the problem, the old "A-Ha" will hit them.

Yes!

Debrief Topics

As mentioned earlier, this activity is a very challenging one. Because of that you may observe some interesting group dynamics. Some topics that might be discussed depending on what happened in your group(s) include:

- **Leadership:** Did you find it easier with just one leader providing directions to the group? How was this person chosen? Was it whoever had an idea? Was this the best system?

- **Creativity:** How many different ideas were tried? Were people encouraged to share new ideas?

- **Cooperation:** Were new ideas worked with? Were any put down? Did one idea spark another?

- **Frustration:** What happened to the group or some players when an idea didn't work? Did it get worse as time went on? Did anything change as the level of frustration went up (fewer ideas put out, more put-downs, arguing, etc.)? Did anyone rally people together to try again? What motivated people to keep trying even after a few attempts that didn't work?

- **Success:** What were some specific things that helped the group succeed? How did it feel to solve such a difficult problem? What lessons can be learned from it?

Two-by-Four

Looking for a real group brain-teaser? This is the one! Similar to *Traffic Jam*, *Two-by-Four* is a great small group, problem-solving activity that can be done just about anywhere.

How to Play

- The activity needs to be done in groups of eight. Divide these eight people into two groups of four, with each small group having a distinct thing in common; i.e., four males or four females, four with blue shirts, four with blue pants, four holding a book and four with empty hands.

- Make a line of the whole group, shoulder-to-shoulder, facing you. The eight people should be lined up so that they alternate by smaller group (one male, one female, one male, one female, etc.)

- Explain to your group that the objective of the activity is to have them get into a line with all players belonging to the same small group of four and having the same thing in common on one side of the line.

- That seems pretty simple, right? Well, the rules that follow should take care of that:

■ Rules

1) The object of the activity is to complete the problem in the least number of moves. Four is the least that it can be done in, but don't tell them this until they've given it at least one try, or they may get discouraged before they even start.

2) All moves must be made in pairs. The pairs must be made up of two people that are right next to each other (on either side).

3) As a pair moves, they leave an empty spot in the line which must be filled by another pair at some point in time — you can't end up with a gap in the line.

4) Players need to keep facing forward the whole time (you can't pivot or turn around).

5) In case you or the group are ever wondering, the four-move solution looks like this:

Things to Think About

This activity is a real tough one. We've had both adult and youth groups work on it for over an hour. But there's also the occasional person or group that sees the solution right off. Although a good amount of frustration is healthy for a group to deal with once in a while, if they seem to be at the point of turning against one another or beating you up, then we recommend giving them the first move. Although this doesn't make it simple, it gets them on their way. We've also had many groups ask to stop for the day to give them time to work it out on paper so that they could solve it for the next session.

Warp Speed

Warp Speed is a great activity to challenge a group's creativity and problem-solving skills. *Warp Speed* and *Group Juggling* make great back-to-back activities because they are very similar and the pattern of one can be used with the other to save time. *Warp Speed* should be done with groups no larger than fifteen.

Things You'll Need

You will only need one soft object (fleece balls work great, so do tennis balls) and a stopwatch.

How to Play

- *Warp Speed* uses the same pattern of tossing as *Group Juggling*. If you keep the group in the same order after they've completed *Group Juggling*, you are all set to go. If time doesn't allow for these two together and you come back to *Warp Speed* another day, follow the directions from *Group Juggling* in order to create your object-tossing pattern.

- Elect a person with a stopwatch to be the "official timekeeper," a most honorable position. This person can also participate in the activity as well as perform the timekeeping duties.

- Rather than trying to juggle by passing many balls around the circle, in *Warp Speed* you are trying to pass just one around the circle (in the same order) as fast as possible.

- The stopwatch will start when you throw the ball to the person that you, as leader, have been throwing to. After it has gone to each player in the proper order and gets back to you, yell "Stop!" and your official timer will give you the group's current "World Record."

- Ask the group how much faster they think they can complete the entire pattern. They will probably take off a few seconds — giving them an achievable new goal. Give them time to figure out how they are going to remove those few seconds from their current time. Doing things the same way will give them about the same time — something needs to change.

- After the group has met their next goal, ask if they're up for another. Can they get even faster? A little encouragement from you will help.

- Remind players that the *only* rule to the game is that the object needs to pass through the same order of people. Off-the-wall ideas are welcome.

Things to Think About

Although you'd never, under even the most excruciating punishment, want to divulge this solution, it is important for you to know because you will be asked if it is legal. The *Ultimate Warp Speed* solution that we have ever seen is usually accomplished by people rearranging themselves to be in the order that they receive the object. Sometimes they do this by forming a new circle or a line or two lines facing each other. Remember, your only rule said that the object needs to be passed in the same order of people every time. The rules didn't say anything about the people changing places (creative solution #1!). Usually this step will take all kinds of time off the previous record.

Many times, if given enough time and if the group is working well together, they will take this idea one step further by putting their hands together, in order, to form a hand-ramp which they then roll the object down. Depending on the group size, this should get them under one second. But wait, once in a while a group will see one more step. By having each person put just one finger in the ramp they can cut down the surface area by roughly one-fifth (one finger instead of five). Usually this will result in a time that is so fast the timer can't start and stop the watch quickly enough.

Again, we share this solution so that you know that these moves are legal. This is not to say that the finger method *is Warp Speed*. *Warp Speed* is whatever the group decides it is. If they feel great about getting their time under eight seconds and no one in the group can think of another method to try, they have reached their own *Warp Speed*.

Debrief Topics

Most times, a lot of positive things happen for a group during *Warp Speed*. The challenge of getting faster and faster times, combined with the creativity that is shared as group members work with different ideas, makes the process exciting and powerful. When *Warp Speed* is reached (whatever *Warp Speed* is for that group), there is usually a lot of celebrating. This activity can only be done with the ideas of many people being added together, built upon and reworked. You can capitalize on all of this and other things that you saw happen by asking some of the following questions:

- What was your time on the first attempt? What is your final time?

- When did you make a big drop in your time? What happened differently during that run? How did that idea come about? What other ways did new ideas come about?

- Were there times when you combined different people's ideas into one? How did that work?

- Did leadership change throughout the activity or stay with one person? How did it change?

- Did everyone feel involved? Were all ideas listened to by others?

Whiz-Bang

Like *Speed Rabbit*, this activity asks a group to have fun together by playing a goofy game. Ninety-nine times out of a hundred, if you have fun introducing it, they'll have fun doing it, so here's how Susan introduces it.

"Once upon a time there was a man named Steve who, while out riding on his bike, rode into some magical orbs. Seeing that magical orbs are so rare, he grabbed them, put them in his pocket and rode home. Later, when he arrived home, he brought out the orbs to show his wife and the orbs whizzed across the room to her. Steve was so impressed with the orbs' magical powers that he thought that they would be tons of fun to play with in a large group. One warning though, when playing with the orbs be extremely careful — one got broken when Steve's son, Sean, crawled over it. Group members must be extremely serious when playing this game or the orbs might get dropped and broken."

Things You'll Need

Two magical orbs. (Call Steve if you need to borrow his.)

How to Play

- The group stands in a circle.

- The leader should pass the orb as fast as possible to either the person on the left or right. The proper technique for passing the orb is a flick of the wrist in the direction that you want it to go in. When using this technique each person must yell, *Whiz*, as they pass it on. Everyone else must continue passing the orb in this same direction unless...

- Someone blocks the path of the orb — sending it the opposite way from its current direction — by putting a hand straight out and yelling, *Bang*. The direction of the orb is now reversed.

- Each person now has the chance to pass the orb in whatever direction they want when it gets to them. They can Whiz it to send the orb in the same direction that it is currently going in, or they can Bang it to reverse its direction.

Whiz-Bang!

- New piece — After the group has got their whizzing and banging down, you can introduce another way to pass the orb around the circle.

- To pass the orb *across* the circle, a player must make eye contact with the person they wish to pass the orb to and then pass it like a basketball while saying, "Vaaaaavooooom." It has to be nice and long — *Vaaaaaaaaaavoooooooom* — say it right now. We don't care where you are, just do it!! Oh, that was a good one — way to go!

- The players receiving this type of pass must catch the orb by putting their hands in front of them and gently catching it while letting out a pleasant, *Ahhhhhhhhh*. After the catch is completed, the receiver can whiz it to a person beside them or vavoom it to someone else. Of course any whiz or vavoom can be banged. Got it? Good!

Kerplunk-Plink!

- Lastly, after players seem to be getting a handle on all of the different options, dig into your pocket and pull out another magical orb so that you now have two going at the same time. If you have a large group you may want to use even more (just keep track of them — they're too expensive to lose).

Other Ideas

If the group understands Vavooooom and Aaaaaaaahhhh quickly, you can add new words. *Kerplunk* is a great one — the orb is tossed like a basketball, and caught by a player making his arms into a basket and saying a sweet *Plink*. Get creative and add some of your own sounds and ways to toss the orb.

Just in case you are wondering about the orbs — they are invisible and weigh nothing — so they cannot actually be felt or seen, but don't worry, get a group going and the orb will take on magical properties.

Womp-Em

Here's another activity (like *Peek-A-Who*) that helps a group to check in with names. For *Womp-Em* you'll want groups of eight to fifteen people.

Things You'll Need

A *boffer* — A boffer is a soft, ethafoam bat that Project Adventure uses for a number of games and that makes a loud sound but causes no pain when used to whack somebody. See safety note below.

How to Play

- Have the group form a circle (tight).

- Have players sit down with their legs straight out in front of them and their feet towards the center of the circle. One player is selected to be in the middle and is given the boffer. You, as the leader, may want to be the first person in the middle if you think it will help to demonstrate the game.

- Start by going around the circle having all the players say their names. You can skip this step if you have just finished playing

Toss-A-Name Game, Peek-A-Who or some other name game or if they know one another's names well.

- One of the players seated in the circle starts the game by calling the name of another player in the circle. The person in the middle then tries to whack — on the foot — the player whose name was called *before* that player can call someone else's name. If the player in the center taps the person whose name is called before that person can call out another name then the player who got tapped goes into the center. This person now takes over the boffer.

- Other ways players can earn their way into the middle include pulling their feet back to avoid being hit or calling the name of someone not in the group.

- The game begins again when the person who was in the center calls the name of someone in the circle.

- As the leader, monitor the time and the group's energy level. Some groups will love to do this activity for a half-hour. Others may be done after ten minutes.

✚ Safety Note

> While the boffers they sell at Project Adventure are flexible and don't hurt, the person in the middle is to hit the people in the circle in the foot, not the legs or body. If your budget doesn't allow for PA boffers you might find paddles with handles in the children's section of a department store. Also, a rolled up and taped newspaper works well. Be sure to have your advisor or teacher give his or her approval before you use anything.

Other Ideas

Another way to play *Womp-Em*, especially with groups whose members already know each other well, is to have players choose animal names to use instead of their own names. Once everyone has an animal name they cannot change it. (Be sure that no two people have the same animal.) As in the first way of doing *Womp-Em*, start by going around the circle to have everyone say their animal name.

Wordles

Wordles are a nice "rainy day special" — quick to pull out when you've got eight outdoor activities planned but the weather tells you that you need to go to plan B. Of course you wouldn't want to limit your use of *Wordles* to just rainy days. The level of fun has no connection to the amount of precipitation. *Wordles* is a sit-down, large or small group activity that encourages brainstorming and quick thinking. It is also a great way to introduce the problem-solving portion of your program. Since it involves creative thinking, *Wordles* can help groups go beyond their usual ways of thinking and seeing problems — skills that will help them a lot with other problem-solving activities.

How to Play

- Starting off with an example will help you provide clear directions and expectations. Just pick one to show the players.
- Here are a few *Wordles* that we took from other Project Adventure books (the numbers are for order, they are not part of the *Wordle*):

1)   **SIDE SIDE**

2)   **GREENNV**

3)   **LOOK KOOL CROSSING**

4)   **HIS.TORY**

5) $\dfrac{\text{I}}{8}$

6)   **EILN PU**

7) **SIGHT LOVE**
   SIGHT
   SIGHT

8) **VAD ERS**

9) **O! 144**

10) **BAN ANA**

11) **ONCE**
    TIME

12)   **2 UM**
    + 2 UM

13) **T I M E**
    ABDE

14) **ALL** **WORLD**

15) **ONE**
    ONE

16) **DICE**
    DICE

17) **0**
    B.S.
    M.D
    Ph.D.

18) **GROUND**
    FEET
    FEET
    FEET
    FEET
    FEET
    FEET

19) **<u>STAND</u>**
      I

ANSWERS:

1) side by side
2) green with envy
3) look both ways before crossing
4) A period in history
5) I overate
6) line up in order
7) love at first sight
8) space invaders
9) Oh, gross!
10) banana split
11) once upon a time
12) forum
13) long time, no see
14) small world after all
15) one on one
16) paradise
17) 3 degrees below zero
18) 6 feet underground
19) I understand

Other Ideas

One way of using *Wordles* is to break up your group into subgroups of 3–5 players. Give each group a set of *Wordles* written out on index cards or write them out on a blackboard for the whole group to see. See if the groups can figure out each of the *Wordles* and/or see which group can do it in the least amount of time (if you and they are in a competitive mood). Other ways of doing this activity are to have each person work on *Wordles* alone or have the participants work on them as a large group. No matter what method you use, encourage players to have fun and be creative with their thinking.

Building Teen and Adult Partnerships

A Key to Community-Wide Substance Abuse Prevention

By Jim Grout and Marv Klassen-Landis

Updated by Steve Fortier

This article first appeared in "New Designs for Youth Development," (Fall, 1989) a journal published by Associates for Youth Development in Tucson, Arizona, USA. It was updated in May, 1994 to reflect new developments in the program.

Substance abuse educators and prevention experts received a troubling report in 1989. According to a November article in the *Wall Street Journal*, teen drug and alcohol use has remained rampant on the Bainbridge Island, Washington, despite 12 years of one of the most extensive drug and alcohol education programs in the country. Student polls revealed that 5% of the junior high and high school students are chemically dependent and that 70% use drugs or alcohol weekly. Substance abuse experts say that the community is typical of other communities across the United States, except for the presence of a model first-through-twelfth-grade substance abuse curriculum. The superintendent of the schools said of the findings, "I'm not sure there is a drug education program in this country that can make a difference. Society is too big an opponent." To carry this further, no drug education program alone can change teens' behavior with substance use. There must be additional involvement of parents and the whole community.

Students Can't Do It Alone

Schools can not bear the sole responsibility for meeting the challenge of adolescent substance abuse. Communities must approach substance abuse prevention as a community responsibility, a community challenge, a community opportunity. The Leadership Project, a National Demonstration Grant Program funded by the Office of Substance Abuse Prevention (OSAP), has found that teams of committed teens and adults are effective catalysts for community-wide substance abuse prevention efforts.

Prevention Programs — Teen Centered or Adult Centered?

Teen alcohol and other drug prevention programs have tended to concentrate either on adult efforts or teen efforts. Adult-centered programs have typically emphasized implementing discipline policies and educating teens about the dangers of substance use. The strengths that adults have brought to such programs are their experience and training, their long-term commitment and availability and their abilities to allocate resources and to organize extensive networks.

The teen-centered peer counseling and peer education approaches to prevention that emerged in the late 1970s and early 1980s drew on young people's enthusiasm and were based on the realization that concerned teens are effective communicators and valuable role models. The teen-centered programs have done good work in training young people in prevention education and in creating alternative, substance-free activities.

One temptation for adults, even in the teen-centered approaches, is to assign teens the roles of implementing adult-designed strategies. Another pitfall in both approaches has been the temptation to view alcohol and other drug use as a teen problem that will be solved by encouraging or enforcing teen behavior changes. Adults need to remember that teens are responding to the fast-paced, pleasure-oriented society they live in. The causes of teen substance use lie in the society which adults have created and which adults, even more than teens, have the power to change. Alcohol and other drug use and abuse are problems throughout our society, and the most effective solution must be built through partnerships between adults and teenagers.

■ Adult and Teen Contributions: Both Are Needed

Teens understandably are hesitant to stand up in a high school assembly and say, "We are for stricter drug and alcohol policies." However, in private, many students say, "Of course, you need clearer, more consistent policies. But don't put that on us. That's your role." A student once remarked, "It's so frustrating! Don't adults understand anymore that kids need discipline, that they need structure? Whatever happened to that idea?" While few admit it in public, teens look to adults for guidance, discipline and direction. If adults become more conscious of the examples they provide as parents and take a more active role in improving the messages our culture gives to children and teenagers, the habits of teenagers will reflect the change. And if adults enter into partnerships with teens, they can contribute experience, resources, and power far beyond that which is normally available to teens.

Teens bring energy, openness and enthusiasm to a teen-adult partnership. They usually have a clearer understanding of the actual attitudes and experiences of their peers than adults have, and at times they are willing to raise challenging questions that adults are reluctant to ask. They have access to their peers and, when they choose healthier lifestyles and get involved in building healthier communities, they show both teens and adults that teens are capable agents of change.

The Leadership Project's Partnership Approach

The first step the Leadership Project took in addressing teen substance abuse in Brattleboro, Vermont and three other towns in Vermont and Massachusetts was to gather together groups of teens and adults who represented a broad range of the social groups in their schools and communities. An effort was made to include young people with varying drug and alcohol attitudes and habits since statistics show that 90% of the seniors in the United States use substances to some degree. The Leadership Project staff asked the teens and adults two questions, "Do you believe that drug and alcohol use is causing problems for today's young people, and do you want to do something about it?" In each town, the staff formed Project Teams of 20 to 25 teens and adults who answered "yes" to both questions. The teen to adult ratio was three to one. The teens represented a broad cross-section; an adult member of one of the teams said, "We have ex-heavy users, straight arrows, jocks, any label you can think of!" In Brattleboro the adult members also reflected diverse professional and personal backgrounds including the local high school health teacher, an adolescent addictions counselor, a few parents and a recovering addict.

■ The Project Teams

The first task of the team was to involve other community members in helping them to identify the causes and to propose potential solutions to teen alcohol and other drug use. Using the Youth Opportunity Planning Process (Lofquist, 1983), the Brattleboro Leadership Project Team involved sixty local residents- thirty teenagers and thirty adults- in this needs assessment process. After identifying the factors contributing to the use of alcohol and other drugs by local young people the group then identified efforts which were already present which addressed the factors and developed other potential solutions that addressed the causes rather that the symptoms. In Brattleboro, some such ideas included creating consistent and equitable community drug and alcohol policies, providing more affordable, substance-free activities for both adolescents and families and developing opportunities for better communication. Teens and adults agreed that communities should encourage dialogue across social and economic groups, age groups and school cliques. They also felt that people of all ages needed emotional support, positive role models, and increased self-esteem, trust and a sense of belonging within the community.

■ Building Teen/Adult Partnerships

The project teams agreed to serve both as a model of teen-adult partnerships and as catalysts for healthy changes in their communities. A Leadership Project coordinator provided leadership for each project team. An important part of the coordinators' role was to communicate the following messages equally to teens and adults:

We are leaders and potential leaders. Our ideas and actions can change the community.

We come from a variety of backgrounds and perspectives, and we're not always going to agree. Partnership doesn't mean that conflicts disappear; our partnership is an opportunity to face the struggles and conflicts, to stick it out and make long-range commitment to building a healthier community.

There won't be instant successes or instant results. We will need to keep our eyes on our major goals and remember that it will take years, not days or weeks, to achieve them.

Coordinators also encourage the adults to adopt the following attitude towards young people:

You probably know more about the causes of the substance abuse problem and about the needs of teenagers than I do. You need to help me to understand. As a 39-year-old, I cannot see the world through the eyes of a 15-year-old. You need to tell me what your world is like, and I'll help you understand the world I experience and have experienced in the past. Together, we'll find ways to create solutions.

■ It Isn't Easy

Developing effective teams from diverse groups of teens and adults has not been easy. After one difficult session, one teen remarked, "Now I understand why all of these groups don't hang out together!" The adults found that partnership with teens required adopting a new stance; most had related to teens primarily as a parent, teacher, coach or counselor. They needed to suppress their tendency to immediately to take charge. They also needed to learn to put aside a tendency to label certain students. Apparently failure-bound students emerged as leaders when adults and other teens valued their contributions. The teens had to struggle against a tendency to see adults as merely embodying an authority role–parent, teacher or cop. The process required patience, but as teens and adults worked together for a common cause, each team member learned to see the others as people who care about young people and about their community.

The Leadership Project Coordinators used a variety of Project Adventure techniques and activities to help break down the barriers between the Team members, to enhance communication and trust and to develop a respect for both the differences and similarities between one another. At an early team workshop, one of the Project Team members, a teen recovering from substance dependency said, "Today we are lighting the spark that will grow into a flame." This sense of hope — the strong belief that together they could have a real impact on drug and alcohol problems — and positive responses from their communities enabled the Project Teams to work through interpersonal and intergenerational issues and to build effective teams.

■ The Project Team's Prevention Activities

As the teams developed and implemented their strategies for creating prevention programs and activities in their communities, they brought together the wisdom, the energy, and the skills of both teens and adults. With each strategy, teens and adults shared in the brainstorming and planning, but they found that some tasks were most effectively accomplished by teens and others by adults.

One of the Project Trams' first missions was to communicate the degree of the severity of teen substance use and of the need for prevention to the adults in the community. Generally, adult perspectives are based on their own experiences as young people, with some adjustment from impressions formed from the media. As a result, adults tend to underestimate the levels of adolescent drug and alcohol abuse, and there is often a tendency to assume that "it's not happening in my family, in our schools or in our community." Adult team members made arrangements for presentations at adult groups such as the Rotary and the Kiwanis, social agencies, school faculties and parent groups. They also helped the teenagers prepare for the presentation. But the teens did the majority of the speaking. The impact is stronger, and the crisis and the needs are more apparent when teenagers speak of their actual experiences.

The project teams have also been involved in drug and alcohol education in the elementary and grade schools, another example of joint teen and adult efforts. The teens and adults agreed on the need for educating younger children, and they discussed different strategies for meeting that need. Adult team members arranged the program, an adult-designed curriculum (originally intended for implementation by classroom teachers) was selected and adults trained the teens, but the teens taught the classes to the younger children. The teen's involvement greatly enhanced the credibility of the messages, and the teens provided the children with models of older students making healthy choices.

Youth/Adult Dialogs

To meet their goal of developing dialogue between community members, the project teams implemented Dialogue Nights. Originally designed by Ron Gaetano to encourage communication between teens and parents, Dialogue Nights provide a structured forum to help adults and youths understand each other's experiences and perceptions. Dialogue Nights focus on specific themes such as exploring personal values, the nature of healthy relationships, the qualities of good listening and attitudes about issues such as choice of friends, school and work pressures and drug and alcohol issues. The Project Teams went on to develop formats that encourage teens and police and teens and teachers to explore their expectations of each other and their common goals. The teens facilitate the Dialogue Nights' small group discussions. Having the teen in charge of encouraging adults to open up and discuss important issues is an unexpected and effective role reversal.

Student Assistance Programs

Both teens and adults pointed to the need for school programs that identify and support students with drug and alcohol or other personal problems. Because of the discipline and intervention orientation of such student assistance programs, adults took responsibility for implementing the programs. The teens, however, added a new dimension. They said, "Support shouldn't be completely crisis-oriented. Why wait until problems become severe? If confidential, supportive services were available, we would use them." As a result, the guidance department at Brattleboro Union High School changed its mission and structure. It has moved away from scheduling and career counseling as its main activities to providing more student discussion groups and other support services. The department also changed its name to "Counseling and Health Services" and its structure to incorporate the school nurse and health teacher. In partnership with students, the local youth service bureau and several mental health agencies, this department has developed discussion groups which provide confidential, adult-facilitated forums for students to share their thoughts and feelings about concerns such as peer acceptance, family issues, dating, friendships, school pressure and drug and alcohol issues.

Community-Wide Prevention

The project teams also have worked together to develop and sponsor parenting classes, drug-and alcohol-free activities, Project Adventure personal and group development programs in the schools and communities, community-wide substance awareness campaigns and Link-Up Rallies. The Link-Up Rallies have brought hundreds of people together to celebrate their communities' growing support for and involvement in prevention efforts. One of the more recent developments in the program has been training Leadership Project Team members in the high school and at several Brattleboro elementary schools to lead Project Adventure team building activities for their peers and adult groups (including the Brattleboro Police Department). This program seeks to help people of all ages to appreciate themselves and others and to view challenges as opportunities for growth.

The partnerships that the teens and adults have demonstrated in the Brattleboro Leadership Project Team are constantly expanding as teens, parents, educators, police, social services and community groups band together to build community-wide prevention networks.

The Leadership Project was founded on the premise that substance abuse prevention is a community responsibility and an opportunity for growth. The teen and adult volunteers who make up the Brattleboro Leadership Project Team have translated this premise into action. As a result, in a five-year period, over 5,000 people have participated in prevention activities ranging from attending teen-adult dialogues and drug and alcohol awareness presentations and rallies to creating student assistance programs and forming community prevention coalitions that include teens, parents, educators, counselors, police officers and community leaders. Working in partnership, small groups of teens and adults have ignited the sparks that continue.

The Leadership Project, a program of Project Adventure, Inc., offers train-the-trainer workshops for those interested in using its program ideas and experiences. In 1990, The Leadership Project was selected as one of ten Exemplary Prevention Programs in the United States by three national organizations. Since the time of the initial writing of this article, Project Adventure has trained over one thousand adult and youth leaders in The Leadership Project concepts and activities. For more information on these training services, call Project Adventure's Vermont office at 802-254-5054.

Jim Grout is founder of The Leadership Project. and current Director of Project Adventure's Vermont office. Marv Klassen-Landis, a free-lance writer, also contributed to the initial writing of this article.

Project Adventure
Services and Publications

Services

Project Adventure, Inc. is a national, non-profit corporation dedicated to helping schools, agencies, and others implement Project Adventure programs. Toward that end, the following services are available:

Project Adventure Workshops. Through a network of national certified trainers, Project Adventure conducts workshops for teachers, counselors, youth workers and other professionals who work with people. These workshops are given in various sections of the country. Separate workshops are given in Challenge Ropes Course Skills, Counseling Skills for Adventure Based Programs, Project Adventure Games and Initiatives, and Interdisciplinary Academic Curriculum.

Challenge Course Design and Installation. Project Adventure has been designing and installing ropes courses (a series of individual and group challenge elements situated indoors in a gymnasium or outdoors in a grove of trees) for over 15 years. PA Staff can travel to your site and design/install a course appropriate for your needs and budget.

Challenge Ropes Course Source Book. A catalog service of hard-to-find materials and tools used in the installation of Challenge Ropes Courses. This catalog also contains climbing rope and a variety of items useful to adventure programs.

Executive Reach. Management workshops for business and professional persons. These workshops are designed for increasing efficiency of team members in the workplace. The trust, communication, and risk-taking ability learned in the executive programs translate into a more cohesive and productive team at work.

Program Accreditation. The Accreditation process is an outside review of a program by PA staff. Programs that undertake the accreditation process are seeking outside evaluation with regard to quality and safety. The term accreditation means "formal written confirmation." Programs seeking confirmation are looking to ensure that they are within the current standards of safety and risk management. This assurance may be useful for making changes in program equipment and/or design, and in providing information on program quality to third parties such as administrators, insurance companies and the public.

Publications

If you would like to obtain additional copies of this book, an order form is provided on the next page. Project Adventure also publishes many books and pamphlets in related areas. Described below are some of our best sellers, which can be ordered on the same form. Call or write to Project Adventure for a complete publications list.

Cowstails and Cobras II. Karl Rohnke's classic guide to games, Initiative problems and Adventure activities. Offering a thorough treatment of Project Adventure's philosophy and approach to group activities, *Cowstails II* provides both the experienced practitioner and the novice with a unique and valuable resource.

Silver Bullets. More Initiative problems, Adventure games and trust activities from Karl Rohnke: 165 great games and activities that require few, if any, props. Use this as a companion to *Cowstails and Cobras II* or a stand alone guide to invigorate your program.

Bridges To Accessibility. More doors are opening for disabled and able bodied persons to interact in risk-taking environments. Are we prepared to be proactive in responding to this transition, to look at our own attitudes and *want* to accept persons of all abilities into our programs — including the forty-three million Americans with disabilities who will soon more fully enter the mainstream. *Bridges To Accessibility* provides adventure leaders with a foundation for this integration and includes: an overview of disabilities, appropriate terminology, assessment of program/facility accessibility, resources for training and programming, recent legislation, suggestions for making activities accessible, and more.

Islands Of Healing: A Guide to Adventure Based Counseling. Long a standard in the field, *Islands* presents a comprehensive discussion of this rapidly growing counseling approach. Started in 1974, ABC is an innovative, community-based, group counseling model that uses cooperative games, Initiative problem solving, low and high Challenge Ropes Course elements, and other Adventure activities. The book contains extensive "how-to" information on group selection, training, goal setting, sequencing, and leading and debriefing activities. Also included are explorations of model ABC programs at several representative sites — junior and senior high schools, a psychiatric hospital, and court referred programs.

Please send information on the following programs:

❏ Project Adventure Training Workshops
❏ Challenge Course Design & Installation
❏ Ropes Course Equipment Catalog
❏ Executive Reach Programs
❏ Publications List
❏ Program Accreditation
❏ Please add my name to your mailing list

Qty	Title	Price	Total
	Yth. Leadership in Action	$14.00	
	Cowstails and Cobras II	$20.00	
	Silver Bullets	$20.00	
	Bridges to Accessibility	$14.00	
	Islands of Healing	$20.50	

Subtotal

5% tax (Mass. residents only) _____

Shipping (instructions below) _____

Total _____

Shipping instructions:
Orders up to $35.00 — add $4.00
Orders over $35.00 add 10% of total
(Canada & overseas, add additional $4.00 to total)

Ship To:
Name _____
Street _____
City _____ State _____ Zip _____
Phone (_____) _____

Payment:
❏ Check enclosed   ❏ Purchase Order

Charge to: ❏ MasterCard   ❏ Visa

Card # _____ Exp. Date _____

Signature _____
(signature required for all credit cards)

Copy or detach this form and return to:

Project Adventure, Inc.

P.O. Box 100
Hamilton, MA 01936
TEL 978/468-7981
FAX 978/468-7605

or

P.O. Box 2447
Covington, GA 30015
TEL 770/784-9310
FAX 770/787-7764

Or Call: 800/795-9039